Invited Into Destiny

Finding Your God-given Purpose

Benton J. Ward

This book is dedicated to my wife Megan who has supported my writing and been very patient with me. I love you. Also, thank you to Corinne for reading and editing this book and to the rest of my family and friends who have always been there, challenging and encouraging me to be the best I can be. I love you all.

From The Author

Thanks for reading this book! I hope it will challenge you to view your calling differently and to take the necessary steps to achieve the purpose that God has for you.

I wanted to take a minute to also let you know of something that I am doing with this book. For every book sold, I'm giving half of my profits to a missions/church organization or project. It could be helping a local church youth group or college ministry raise funds to go on their yearly missions trip, a local fund raising endeavor for overseas mission projects, or a new missionary raising funds to go to their specific missions field.

The reason for this decision is because there are people all over the world who don't know Him and have a need that needs to be met in their lives, whether financial, spiritual, physical, etc. This need keeps them from thriving. The purpose of this book is to make disciples of Jesus who are able to thrive in every area of life. Missions is the heart of God. I would love to partner with you or your church missions department to help these people thrive. If you have a specific missions project that you would like to give to financially and want another fundraising method, I would love to partner with you.

How would this work?

My hope is that you or your church would commit to partnering with me to sell this book, not only to see the contents of this book help in the lives of those who read it, but to also help see others all around the world thrive through a financial gift.

To explain what this would look like let me explain the royalties process and how much of my profit would actually go to missions:

- If the book is bought on Amazon my royalties are $4.85. This means that I would give $2.43 to a missions project.
- If the book is bought from me in person for the full price of $15, I would give half of what I profit to a missions project. My print cost for each book is 4.14 plus shipping. So, after factoring in shipping costs, I would give $5 for each book sold to missions.

While I still am planning on giving half of my royalties to missions either way, the ideal scenario would be for me to come to your church and bring books with me to sell directly (such as at a missions banquet, when there is a guest missionary, or if you want to book me to speak at an event) or for you to commit to helping me sell a specific amount (ex: 10 for individuals, 100 for churches) to keep the shipping cost lower and the amount given to missions higher.

Interested?

If you or your church/missions organization are interested in partnering with me to see others thrive in every area of life, please email me at bentonjward.author@ gmail.com to discuss more.

Contents

Introduction

Have you ever wondered what your calling is? Have you ever had a dream that you knew without a doubt was from God, but you just didn't know how it was going to happen because of your lack of knowledge or ability? Welcome to the story of every follower of Jesus, a story that progresses as He reveals who He is and what He has for us.

When we choose to follow Jesus, we begin a journey filled with newfound thrills, but also challenging trials as we experience growth and transformation. Sometimes it's slower than we'd like, and we might not understand it all the time. However, over time, as we seek Him, He gives us a revelation of the person He wants us to become and then transforms us to be like Him.

What holds many of us back is our own limitations, as well as a lack of understanding of His calling. We get so wrapped up in our own goals and plans that we miss or ignore His invitation to step into a higher plan. We miss the deeper things He has for us and the transformation that He intends to do in our lives. As a result, the dreams that God puts in our hearts will never grow because we are not pursuing them. So many people's dreams have died because of this.

This almost happened to me. I've had a few dreams that I've had for a long time. However, I never took the time to pursue and grow in my talents to achieve any of these dreams. Instead, I focused on doing other things that I thought God had told me to do but were just me following my own plans. As a result, those dreams never grew and almost died until God revealed to me that He wanted to grow His kingdom through them. He told me that for me to be the person He had designed me to be I had to let go of my will and follow Him. After realizing this, I surrendered my will and started the journey of simply learning what it means to simply be like Christ. I mentioned a part of this in my first book *Live It. BE It.* Since then, as I've started allowing myself to let go of old mindsets and ways of doing things, God has taught me several principles about calling that I want to share with you in this book. The first is this: our calling foremost is an invitation to journey through life with Him. During this journey He invites us to step into the plan and gifts He has for us that will help transform us into who He has called us to be. It is a journey that is difficult and takes time and a lot of patience and discernment but is worth it because it leads to our destiny. My hope as you read this book is that if you haven't figured out your purpose yet that God would reveal it to you, and that you can live a life thriving in every area as you discover how to follow Jesus the way He wants you to.

PART 1 God's Design

For I know the thoughts that I think toward you, says the LORD, thoughts of peace and not of evil, to give you a future and a hope.

Jeremiah 29:11

Chapter 1

Destiny

What is my destiny? What is my purpose? These are two of the biggest questions that every person on the face of the earth will ask at some point in their life. Destiny is defined by dictionary.com as "something that is to happen or has happened to a particular person or thing; lot or fortune; the predetermined, usually inevitable, or irresistible, course of events, and the reason for which something exists or is done, made, used, etc."[1] I also like how the Merriam-Webster dictionary defines it: "Destiny implies something foreordained and often suggests a great or noble course or end."[2] In other words, our destiny is the purpose we were created for, the goal we strive to achieve before the end of our lives. God planned this destiny for our lives before we were born.

For some people, thinking of God's plan for their lives sometimes causes great anxiety and depression because they feel like they have no destiny or purpose. Others become disillusioned and disheartened because they feel like they have a purpose, but don't understand how they fit into the bigger picture of God's plan and kingdom. Some who are older believe they have failed to achieve their purpose, never fulfilling the dreams that God had given them. They suffer from depression and discouragement because of this mindset.

Some wander around in circles for years chasing dreams, trying to find meaning in life, but never truly being content in anything they do. Failing to find purpose, they become lost and alone in their despair. Some dream big dreams but don't actually pursue those dreams because of insecurities or lack of motivation. Others pursue their own dreams, purposes and plans, not realizing they aren't God's dreams at all. They fail over and over again, wondering why God's not prospering them, but keep getting back up and chasing them anyway because of stubbornness, never realizing they are chasing things that God never intended for them.

I was one of those people walking around in circles trying to find my place in life. I had big dreams that I thought were from God, but were, in reality, my own dreams. Even though I was in ministry, I still refused to acknowledge that what I was doing wasn't what God had created me to accomplish. I suffered from disillusionment that almost brought me down a path of depression if it wasn't for my faith in God and trust that He would direct my steps. However, it still took me letting go of every dream that I had in order to keep from burning out. Letting go helped me to simplify my life so that I could really listen to what He was telling me rather than trying to do a lot to achieve my goals. Doing this helped me to realize two things: first, it helped me to realize what dreams were from God and which ones were my own; and second, which ones that I needed to focus on now versus which ones I could wait on pursuing.

That is what my prayer is for all of you who might be experiencing disillusionment and discouragement about your place in life. If you are like me, wandering around trying to figure out your purpose, my challenge to you is this: stop. Take a break. Quit trying so hard to keep doing what you are doing and just breathe. God does have a plan for you, but sometimes it takes letting go and just simply being with God to figure it out. Learn to walk with Him and just simply be content in your relationship with Him instead of trying to figure it out. I'll talk more about this as I continue this book so keep reading.

STORIES OF DESTINY

When we think about destiny and purpose what comes to mind? We hear stories about heroes and heroines fulfilling their destinies by accomplishing great feats and going on great adventures, slaying dragons, finding suddenly that they have powers that they didn't before and have been chosen to rid the world of some kind of evil. Others get called into another fantastic world to go on a quest that leads to them eventually triumphing over some evil overlord.

For me, a scene in the movie *Empire Strikes Back,* released in 1980, comes to mind. Luke Skywalker is running from Darth Vader and has run into a dead end at a drop into nothingness. Vader gives the infamous revelation that all Star Wars fans know, "Luke, I am your father." He invites Luke to join him in defeating the emperor and to rule the galaxy by his side. To entice Luke to join him, he says, "Luke, it is your destiny." Obviously, Vader thought these words would result in Luke giving up everything to join him. Destiny was a huge part of the Jedi teaching. Of course, evil overlord isn't really that great of a destiny, as we all know what usually happens to them. They usually get overthrown by a mighty force of good and lose everything including their lives most of the time. In the end, in the last episode of the original Star Wars Trilogy, *Return of the Jedi*, Luke Skywalker's destiny ended up being that he did indeed help his father defeat the emperor. However, he didn't accomplish this by joining his father and turning to the dark side of the Force. Instead, he stuck to his core values and beliefs, knowing that the dark side was wrong. He had hope that his father still had good in him and in the end was correct in this assessment. By helping his father realize his love for both him and his sister Leia, Luke fulfilled his own destiny. His destiny was to help his father come back to the light side, defeat the emperor, and restore justice and peace to the galaxy.

Another example of a powerful story of destiny was the story of King Arthur. If you know the story, then you know that there was a sword stuck in a stone. This sword, called Excalibur, was extremely famous for being a powerful magic sword that could give its wielder great power and influence. The legend was that whoever pulled the sword from the stone was the rightful king of Britain and would be the greatest king Britain had ever known. However, the sword was enchanted so that no one but the destined king could pull it out of the stone. Hundreds of powerful knights tried to pull the sword out of the stone. However, they all failed, until a boy named Arthur, the lost son of the former king Uther Pendragon, came one day and pulled the sword out of the stone. He was named king of Britain and became the greatest king Britain had ever seen or would see, ruling the nation well, and was loved by all. He established the famous Knights of the Round Table in his capital city,

Camelot, along with a few well-known knights who were all powerful, well respected and loved by all. Stories of King Arthur and His Knights of the Round Table and their adventures and exploits have been sung and written about for hundreds of years.

There are hundreds of tales such as these; grandiose legends of fantastic wizards, kings, warriors, who all accomplished amazing things. Each of these heroes had a great destiny. Because of how prevalent these stories of destiny and purpose are, our society has given destiny and purpose a sense of mysticism and fantasy. People seek a grand adventure and supernatural life that they can only dream of. Unfortunately, the average person, if they compare their story to these grand stories of destiny and purpose, might think that these stories are unachievable and that they can't have a destiny as great as that. These tales of grand adventures have caused disillusionment in people who believe that these stories are the pinnacle of destiny. Unfortunately, these tales are fantasy.

However, something to remember is that even though these stories might be unreal and farfetched, each of us can have a fantastic and extraordinary story of destiny. We have a story of destiny that we have been created for if we look for it in the right place. We have been created with a destiny that has a lot of potential for us to experience great things that we can only dream of. In this story we can experience growth and transformation that allows us to become the strongest and greatest version of ourselves. We can also experience supernatural things beyond our wildest comprehension that blow all of the fantastic, mostly made up, stories of destiny we hear out of the water.

Our destinies can even allow us to experience rewards that go beyond our lives on this earth, rewards that last for all eternity. Imagine that! A story and destiny where you can become the best, strongest, most confident version of yourself, having the ability to accomplish anything, experience amazing, incomprehensible, supernatural things happening in your life, and seeing results and rewards from your accomplishments even after you die! Sign me up for this story! Some might ask "how is this possible?" The answer is simple and doesn't require you to do anything but have faith; faith in a good God who loves to partner with people to accomplish His perfect plans on the earth. Are you interested in finding out more about this destiny that you can have when you have faith in God? Then keep reading.

Chapter 2

The Perfect Plan

God has created each of us with a divine purpose and destiny in mind. This divine story He has written for our lives has potential for us to experience true transformation, incomprehensible and supernatural things happening around us, and for us to receive rewards in eternity. Jeremiah affirms this in Jeremiah 29:11 when he gives this prophecy from the Lord, "for I know the thoughts that I think toward you, says the Lord, thoughts of peace and not of evil, to give you a future and a hope." God's thoughts towards us and plan for our lives according to this verse is a plan that brings us peace and gives us a future and a hope. Doesn't that sound fantastic? God wants to give us peace, a future, and a hope for eternity. That is the kind of God I personally think is worth following. No other God can provide us with true peace, a future, and a hope for eternity. All other gods require us to do impossible things to earn their favor. Sometimes the things we do for these lesser gods aren't even enough to keep their favor. Why would anyone choose to follow gods who require us to do things that are impossible to do in order to earn their favor?

Some still may be skeptical about this great God who has a fantastic plan. It may seem to be too good to be true. Some might even question the validity and goodness of this kind of God, especially with all of the evil in the world. The best thing about the God I am talking about is that not only does He have a good plan for us, He also helps us achieve the plan He has for us if we partner with Him. You might ask "I thought God was far away and invisible. How does He help us?" I'll answer this throughout this book so keep reading.

There's something else that's exciting about this verse. This verse actually has deeper meaning than what the English translators have interpreted it to mean. As wonderful as peace, a future, and a hope are, there's more to what God is saying in this verse than what we have understood. Something that we all should remember is that the Bible was written in another language besides English. The Old Testament was written in Hebrew and the New Testament was written in Greek. To get a better understanding of this verse's context we need to examine what the original writer was saying in his native language: Hebrew. Let's break down this verse a little bit more and look at the Hebrew to get the full meaning of what God is saying to us.

> *"For I know the thoughts that I think toward you, says the Lord."*

The word "thoughts" in Jeremiah 29:11 in the original Hebrew is the word *maḥăšāḇâ* which, according to the Strong's Hebrew Lexicon means "intentions, plans, inventions, purpose or thought."[1]Another good word we could use to define this word is the word "blueprint." The beginning of this verse shows us that God knows the blueprints, plans, or designs that He has for our lives. If you think about it in engineer or architectural terms, a blueprint, design, or plan for a well-designed piece of equipment or building requires a lot of planning and thought. God's blueprint or design for our lives is the same. Do you ever wonder why the human body is so complex? That's because since the first humans, God has put a lot of thought into how He creates us, forming us intricately and specifically. He also puts a lot of thought into the destiny He has for us, the purpose for which we were created. We are intricately and wonderfully designed, each of us a masterpiece from the Master Creator, uniquely formed and designed with a specific, well thought out purpose. I will talk about this more in depth in a later chapter. For now, let's go to the next part of this verse.

"Thoughts of Peace and Not of Evil"

The word "peace" in the second part of this verse has been defined in English as "a state of tranquility or quiet, harmony in personal relations, a state or period of mutual concord between governments, or a pact or agreement to end hostilities between those who have been at war or in a state of enmity." [2] While this definition is definitely a great interpretation of this scripture and can bring hope for our lives, it is not a complete translation. The word used in this verse that we translate as peace is the word *šālôm* in the original Hebrew. While the Hebrew definition includes what we know of as peace: "peace, quiet, tranquility, contentment," "peace, friendship" implying friendship in

9

human relationships and with God, and "peace from war", it actually is more accurately defined as "completeness, safety or soundness in body, and welfare, health, and prosperity." [3]

So, to give us a better understanding of what God is saying in this part of the verse it would be better translated and understood this way: His blueprint and design for our lives is that we

1. are complete in Him because everything we need is found in Him,
2. have security and soundness in life because He keeps us safe emotionally, physically, mentally etc. when we follow Him,
3. are healthy in every area of life; physically, mentally, emotionally, relationally, financially, etc., because He gives us health, heals us when we are sick, and also gives us the ability to prosper and thrive in every area of life,
4. have peace, quiet, tranquility, and contentment when we are with Him and follow Him,
5. have peace in all relationships and in every situation including war, because of Him giving us favor with everyone including our enemies.

Wow! How awesome is this! Are you intrigued by the plans that God has for you yet? I am! Let's keep going.

"To Give You a Future and A Hope"

This ending to Jeremiah 29:11 is self-explanatory. The words "future" and "hope" that we understand are good translations from the Hebrew, allowing us to see and understand that God wants us to have a future and a hope. Let's examine it closer and think about it more for a second before we continue so that we can let this statement sink in.

The way God says this statement allows us to gain a perfect understanding of God's designs and purpose for our lives. Simply put, God wants us to have a future with Him and a hope in Him. Not just that, but when examined through the lens of Scripture as a whole as we read other passages in the Bible, we see that God doesn't want us to just have a normal future. He wants us to have an amazing future with Him. Paul tells us in Ephesians that He is a God "who is able to do exceedingly abundantly above all that we ask or think, according to the power that works in us." This is God's heart for us. He wants to do more in and through us than we can think or imagine. He wants to work everything for our good according to Romans 8:28. God didn't create us and then leave us hanging on our own as some believe. He has a destiny in mind for us that includes giving us a bright future filled with incredible experiences and a hope that we can spend eternity with Him. I will talk more about this in later parts of this book.

Are you still with me? I hope so! This verse is such a powerful illustration of what God's heart is for us. To allow us to gain a better understanding of what God is telling us in Jeremiah 29:11, all of these definitions should be added into this verse. Let's take a look at what God is telling us in this paraphrase that includes the above definitions:

> "For I know the blueprints and purposes that I have carefully and thoughtfully designed, intended, and planned for your lives, says the Lord. I have amazing plans intended for you, not of evil, but for you to experience completeness, wholeness, security, health, quiet, tran-

quility, and contentment in every area of your life. These plans will allow you to thrive and be prosperous in every area of life: physically, emotionally, mentally, relationally, and financially. My intention with these plans is to give you a bright and better future and a hope."

Jeremiah 29:11

Wow! Put this way this well-known verse shows the greatness and goodness of God! It brings His thoughts towards us to life, allowing us to understand His plan better than before. This is the kind of God I want to serve! However, understanding His plans might still be difficult for us to comprehend, unfortunately, because it does take a level of faith in what we cannot see. God very rarely reveals His full plans to His people. This can be frustrating at times because we're impatient, wanting to know things immediately. Fortunately, He reveals His plans a little bit at a time to those who follow Him, just at the right time. It just won't be the way we might want it to be. This means that if we want to learn His will, we must build a relationship with Him.

Having a relationship with God requires us to seek Him, relentlessly, and with all that we have in order to know who He is. When we have a relationship with Him and have learned to listen to Him, we can learn what His design for our life is. We can then learn how to accomplish the purpose He created us for. Jeremiah emphasizes this in the next few verses after Jeremiah 29:11. He tells us in verse 13, "and you will seek Me and find Me, when you search for Me with all of your heart." Seeking Him with all of our heart is the only way for us to find Him and find our true, eternal destinies.

LESSER PLANS

Unfortunately, there are times when we choose not to seek Him. We choose to do things our own way, following lesser plans. This, unfortunately, is human nature. Because of sin we are naturally prone to follow our own selfish desires instead of turning to God. Those who don't pursue God will never find their divine destiny, a destiny that is only found in Him. Those who don't pursue God will always settle for lesser designs. These lesser plans might seem good and can give us a sense of purpose for a time. However, they are imperfect and corrupt. They will never last. Because of this corruption they will eventually fall short of true, lasting, eternal purpose and eventually lead to our destruction. They will also never truly give us the hope for eternity that only life with God offers.

We see that this was the very reason that God spoke the words of Jeremiah 29:11 to the prophet Jeremiah in the first place. To give this verse a bit of historical context we have to look at who Jeremiah was and what was happening during his life. Born to the family of a priest during the reign of the evil King Manasseh, Jeremiah, called the weeping prophet, was the prophet to the nation of Judah. He prophesied throughout the periods of time just before and during the Babylonian conquest of Judah. He was sent by God to warn the people of Judah of the upcoming judgment that He was about to use Babylon to bring upon the nation. After the conquest of Babylon where Judah was destroyed and thousands of Hebrews were captured and brought to Babylon, God used him to bring words of encouragement and hope of restoration to the nation if they would repent and turn to Him.

Despite Jeremiah's prophetic warnings before the judgment, the people chose to follow their own ways of doing things and their own gods instead of repenting and turning to God. They chose the lesser, imperfect plan that would lead to their destruction. As a result of their disobedience, idolatry, and rebellion, God allowed Babylon to conquer Judah. The walls of the city were completely destroyed, as well as the temple of the Lord and parts of the city itself. Many were captured in this attack and brought to Babylon. Jeremiah prophesied that Judah would remain in captivity for 70 years. However, he also reminded the people that this was never God's design for them and if they would seek Him with all of their hearts, they would find Him and He would restore them to their land.

We see through the lens of biblical history the reason God spoke this prophecy through Jeremiah in Jeremiah 29:11 and 13. God wanted His people to know that His design for them was better than what they were experiencing. The choice to follow their own plan led to their destruction because it wasn't a lasting perfect design. His plan was a plan that would bring them completeness, wholeness, security, health, quiet, tranquility, and contentment, in every area of their lives. His plans would allow them to thrive and be prosperous in every area of life: physically, emotionally, mentally, relationally, and financially. His plan was designed to give them a future and a hope. He went on to graciously remind them that, in spite of their failings and rebellion, His plan could still be achieved. They could be restored to their nation and to a relationship with Him if they would seek Him and turn to Him with all of their hearts.

The same is true for us today. Many in today's society are trying to find their purpose by following their own imperfect blueprints and plans. They are led by their own desires and emotions, following imperfect dreams and plans that constantly change depending on their circumstances. This has caused many to become discouraged because they simply can't accomplish what they want to accomplish. They chase empty dreams and purposes that will never fill the desires in their heart for something greater than themselves. Some might even fall prey to the suffering that life brings them and never pursue a purpose at all, overwhelmed by their own failures, pain, and suffering. They feel like they can't escape what they are going through and have given up all hope. In either case it was because they followed an imperfect, incomplete plan.

INCOMPLETE PLANS

Plans that we make are always destined to fail because they are incomplete. We are finite and limited because we are within time, instead of outside of it. We can't possibly understand how to design our lives perfectly. We can't see the big picture. As a result, when we plan our lives, we won't be able to fully account for every detail that could happen to us. There will always be variables that will be unexpected because we have limited knowledge and understanding. We can't see or understand how the experiences we will endure, how the relationships we build, or the knowledge that we gain will shape us into the people we will become.

God, however, is omnipresent, omniscient, and omnipotent, meaning He is everywhere at the same time, all knowing, and all powerful. He is outside of time and can see all the details of our lives past, present, and future. He knows everything about us and the world we live in. After all He created everything and set every element of our lives into motion. When He is planning our lives and intentionally thinking about who He wants us to be, He considers every detail that will affect our lives. He takes into account how relationships and experiences, both positive and negative, play a part in our development. He also sees how the things taught in our school systems, colleges, and even churches will affect our beliefs, core values, and daily practices. Because He is all powerful, none of these things can change His plans for us except for our choice to disobey Him. After all, He is a God of love who chooses to give us free will. However, even our choices don't affect His plans. He is still sovereign. His eternal plan will still be accomplished. We just won't be a part of it if we choose not to be.

THE SIN FACTOR

Another factor that demonstrates our inability to perfectly plan our own lives is sin. Even though we were created perfectly by God, in His perfect image, because of Adam and Eve's choice to disobey God, sin entered the world, bringing corruption and eternal separation from Him. This corruption caused the perfect image of God within us to be twisted into something it wasn't designed to be. I'll talk more about this in a later chapter. Because of the twisting of our character, we are now ruled by what Paul in Romans calls our "flesh" or the selfish desires within us to do our own thing instead of God's. This corruption affects our own plans for our lives, causing our plans to become twisted and leading us to destruction.

Fortunately, God is perfect. Evil cannot exist within Him. His plans cannot be corrupted by evil. Therefore, His plans are perfect and will always lead to a better future and hope, completeness, wholeness, security, health, quiet, tranquility, contentment, and the ability to thrive in every area of life with Him.

This is the kind of God I want to serve. I have seen the results and consequences of following my own incomplete and imperfect plans, the chaos my bad decisions created within my life. I'm sure most of you could agree. Following our own plan is not worth it. Following God's plan is. Ever since I let go of my own plans and learned to follow His completely, I have experienced peace and contentment in a way that I have never experienced before. He has shown Himself strong in my life, giving me the desires of my heart in a way that blows my mind. His plan is good and worth following. I hope that you will choose to let go of your own ways as well if you haven't yet and follow Him. Let's continue.

Chapter 3

The Invitation

Settling for an imperfect plan and accepting less than God has to offer was never God's intentions for us. God has a purpose for everyone. It's a purpose that is beyond anything we can comprehend, and He wants to reveal it to everyone living and breathing. His plan and destiny for our lives is perfect and worth pursuing.

So many people go through life without knowing their purpose, and as a result, wander around aimlessly without joy or hope. Sometimes even those who believe in Him struggle for years because they have a false, unrealistic understanding of what His plans are for their lives. Some people over-spiritualize their purpose, believing that to find their "calling" they have to have a dramatic revelation, altar experience, or prophetic word to receive God's direction for their lives.

Church culture and leadership in the past have also overemphasized the role of the ministry leader to those they are teaching, not teaching that there is much more to God's intentions for all of us, not just those "called into ministry." It's important to remember that those who aren't chosen to be in a ministry leadership position have a divine purpose too. Everyone has a part to play in God's kingdom and how He establishes it on the earth. We are all called and have a purpose. Not teaching this principle keeps people from experiencing the life God has designed them for. When they don't understand God's plan they are not able to thrive in every area of life.

So how can we find our God given destiny? How can we find true hope and find a life of purpose that can only come from following Jesus? Understanding "calling" is the key to understanding the purpose that God has for us.

CALLED

So, what is calling? As I said before, the church has over-spiritualized this word to the degree where people have misinterpreted what it means to be "called." This has resulted in disillusionment and sometimes even disheartenment and depression. Some misinterpret God's purpose for their lives because they didn't understand what He was calling them to do, starting a career that they were never meant to be in in the first place. This is extremely dangerous for those who mistakenly believe they are called into a ministry role, but don't actually have the calling, talent, or anointing of God to be in a ministry role. Being in a ministry leadership role without having the calling and ability of a pastor, teacher, evangelist, etc. can actually harm the people underneath this leader. It can also damage the life of the leader himself/herself. Most leaders who aren't actually called into ministry will eventually fall into ministry failure or personal depression because they don't have the blessing of God to support them. It's the same in any calling or career. If you aren't actually designed and equipped to do something, then you shouldn't do it. I'll talk more about this in a later chapter.

To understand calling we need to again go back to the Bible to examine the full context. We must examine what the authors meant in the original language. The word "call" in the Greek, the original language of the New Testament, is the word *kaleō* which means to "call aloud, utter in a loud voice, to name, to call by name, to give a name to, to invite by name, to salute by name."[1] Peter uses this word in 1 Peter 2:9 when he says,

> "but you are a chosen generation, a royal priesthood, a holy nation, His own special people, that you may proclaim the praises of Him who called you out of darkness into His marvelous light" (NKJV).

This word has a few implications for us that we must see in order to understand it better. Let's take a look at three of them.

God knows your name.

For someone to call and invite you they must know your name. To put it into terms we can understand, let's look at the modern cell phone. How can someone who doesn't know your name call you and ask to speak to you? They can't. It would be a pointless call or possibly a prank call, which is still pointless. Another example we can use is the wedding invitation. How can someone invite a friend to their wedding if they don't know their name and address? Again, they can't.

The same applies to us in our calling from God. Does God call and invite people without knowing them? No! It's quite the opposite in fact! The One who calls and invites us into His plan knows us! He knows our names! He knows our stories! He knows everything about us because He created us. He knows the designs and plans for our lives and what purpose we'll achieve.

God's Calling is Intentional.

The second implication is this: the call is intentional. There has to be a reason for calling someone otherwise the call is useless. In today's society we have cell phones that we call and text from. There is usually a reason that we call our friends and family. God's calling and invitation is the same. He has an intention and a reason for calling us by name and inviting us.

God's call is an invitation into His plan.

Let's examine this further by looking again at the example of 1 Peter 2:9. Peter perfectly illustrates how God invites us into our purpose when he says, "But you are a chosen generation, a royal priesthood, a holy nation, His own special people, that you may proclaim the praises of Him who called you out of darkness into His marvelous light" (NKJV). This is a great summary of the destiny that we have in God and explains beautifully how God calls us. We are chosen, a royal priesthood, and a holy people, set apart for His purposes.

I want to paraphrase this verse a little bit from a different perspective applying this definition of the word *kaleō* to really bring this verse to life for us. When we truly understand the implications of this verse, we can truly understand how God is inviting us into His plans and what our destiny is. This is what He is saying to us:

> "Where before you were lost in darkness and were alone, orphaned, and corrupted by sin, I invited you by name into a greater purpose. I extended an invitation to you, inviting you to leave the darkness and step into My marvelous light. My invitation to you was also an invitation for you to find freedom, a new name as my son and daughter, and for you to become like Me. Those of you who responded to My invitation are set free from sin. I made you holy and pure like I am holy and pure. I made you my own, giving you a royal identity as My son and daughter, and a title as ruler with Jesus in My kingdom. Now sing my praises, declaring to those around you what I have done. This is your purpose and destiny."

> — 1 Peter 2:9

Again, wow! How great is the plan and the destiny that God has for those who follow Him! How wonderful are His thoughts towards us! He is worth following and His plan is worth pursuing! He is calling us by name and extending an invitation for us to join Him in building His eternal kingdom and experience things beyond our imagination as His chosen, holy, pure, royal people!

ACCEPT THE INVITATION

God calls us by name and extends an invitation to us for one reason: so that we can find Him and find our purpose in Him. God is extending this invitation to everyone through His Holy Spirit. His Holy Spirit convicts those who don't know Him of sin (John 16:8), extending an invitation for them into a journey with Him that will lead to their destiny and freedom. He is calling those of us who do know Him into a deeper walk with Him, inviting us into more of Him. However, in order to accept this invitation, we must have faith; faith in an unseen God who is mysterious but knowable, infinite but close to us, never leaving us or forsaking us. We must have faith to know that He exists and is good; faith to trust that He is faithful to do what He says He will do and "rewards those who earnestly seek Him" (Hebrews 11:6, NKJV).

Faith is hard, especially when you don't understand what God wants. It requires action even if you can't see what's happening or who you're following. That's what leads a lot of people to take their own path. They don't have the faith or trust in God because they can't see why they should follow Him. They have either never experienced Him or are unwilling to submit to Him as Lord. How many of us are like that? Even those of us confessing to be Christians have this issue sometimes.

However, accepting God's invitation into His plan so that you can find your destiny is worth it. He has proven over and over that He is faithful. Ask anyone who has been following Jesus for very long. God has never let us down. If you step out in faith, you will experience a supernatural life of transformation and destiny beyond anything you can comprehend. It is a journey filled with joy, peace, love, hope, and freedom.

If you're anxious, depressed, lonely, angry, have experienced any kind of hurt or pain, or are struggling with finding your purpose, I invite you to step out in faith and accept God's invitation that He is extending out to you today. Seek Him with all of your heart so that you can find

Him and know Him. If you've followed Him for a while, but are experiencing confusion about your calling or are experiencing some kind of disappointment, I invite you to accept the invitations that God is extending to you throughout this book. He knows you, knows your struggles, knows your dreams and hopes, and wants you to find wholeness, peace, and contentment in Him. He wants to be your firm foundation so that when you do go through hard times, you can remember to rest in Him.

Over the next few chapters, I will discuss principles that will help you to understand your destiny better and hopefully help you discover a newfound or revitalized faith in God. The first principle is this. An invitation into your destiny is an invitation into a story.

Chapter 4

Invited Into A Story

Over the last two chapters, I have introduced the topic of destiny. God has a well thought out destiny for you. He has formed and designed this plan for you since before you were born; a plan to experience completeness, wholeness, security, health, quiet, tranquility, and contentment, in every area of your life. How do we figure out this destiny? By hearing and responding to His calling.

Calling is simply an invitation. God is inviting every person on earth by name to step into this destiny with Him. The Holy Spirit convicts us of sin before we know Jesus (John 16:8) and invites us into a relationship with Him; to know Him, believing in our hearts and confessing with our mouths that Jesus is Lord (1 John 1:9). He also invites those who follow Him into a life of more. If you step out in faith and respond to His invitation into this perfect plan, He will give you what you need to thrive in every area of life: physically, emotionally, mentally, relationally, financially, as well as give you a future and a hope. As part of His plans and purposes for your life, He wants you to experience freedom and transformation, see supernatural things happen around you that will be beyond your comprehension, and reap eternal reward.

However, this journey to our destiny is a process. To understand this process, we must understand the elements that He invites us into. These elements are crucial parts of our journey that help us find and achieve our destiny. To help us along this journey it's important to realize that God is inviting us into a story that has lasted since the beginning of time.

THE ETERNAL STORY

Stories have different parts with different themes that ultimately lead to an ending. The beginning of most stories of destiny introduces a hero or heroine before they find their destiny. In most fantasies or adventure stories the hero or heroine is usually someone average or even below average who experiences something that will launch them into a grand adventure filled with wonder, mystery, and challenges that they have to overcome. As the story progresses, the hero or heroine experiences transformation that allows them to achieve their destiny. They go through trials that push them beyond their limits, making them stronger. As they face these challenges, they gain confidence in their abilities, growing more power as the story progresses. Some of these heroes/heroines have someone in their lives, or someone they meet along the way, who helps them find their courage or trains them to overcome the obstacles. By the end of the story they are powerful, confident, influential people who have overcome any obstacle they faced and have accomplished the tasks set before them. They have achieved their destiny.

An example of this is from the classic Chronicles of Narnia book: *the Lion, Witch, and the Wardrobe,* written by C.S. Lewis. The story begins with four children, the Pevensies, who live in England during World War II. Peter, the oldest, is thirteen years old, Susan the oldest girl, is twelve, Edmund, the youngest boy, is ten, and Lucy, the youngest, is eight years old. They get evacuated from London and sent to live with Digory Kirke, an eccentric professor who lives by himself in a huge mansion in the English countryside. One rainy day, while playing hide and seek, Lucy stumbles upon a wardrobe that she uses to hide from her siblings. Unbeknownst to her, this wardrobe is magical. It is a doorway into another world called Narnia. Lucy finds Narnia and a new friend, a fawn named Mr. Tumnus. However, none of her siblings believed her story when she came back. They believed instead that she had made up the story about a fantastic new world to get attention. The second time Lucy goes through the wardrobe, Edmund secretly follows her, hoping to catch her in the lie and make fun of her. However, he stumbles through as well after her. Unfortunately, he was too far behind her and instead of meeting Mr. Tumnus, he meets the evil white witch, queen of Narnia. Falling under her spell after the temptation of more candy and to be made a prince, he promises to bring all of his siblings to her, not knowing that she intended to kill them.

All four of the children eventually end up in Narnia and learn of their destiny to become the kings and queens of Narnia and end the spell of eternal winter that the nation has been under, cast by the white witch. However, Edmund joins the white witch betraying the children, while the others seek Aslan, who is the lion God of Narnia. Over the course of the story, we see the progression of the children as they learn of their destiny, find Aslan, discover who he is, help Edmund to gain freedom, battle against the white witch's army to destroy her curse, witness Aslan's death, resurrection, and triumph over the white witch, and eventually their growth into the kings and queens they were destined to be with the help of Aslan and their friends.

Another great story we can use as an example is the story of Disney's *Mulan*. Mulan was born in the nation of China, the daughter of an old, disabled war hero. The nation was about to go to war with the Hun army and was calling all of the men who were capable of fighting to join the army to face them. The problem was that Mulan's father was disabled. He could not fight, but was still required to go. Fearing for her father, Mulan wanted to go in his place. However, in that time women could not join the Chinese army. Still, Mulan was determined to save her father. She decided to disguise herself as a man and join the army. Throughout the course of her training, she endured physical and emotional challenges because of her physical limitations as a girl. But with the help and encouragement of her tiny guardian spirit, the dragon Mushu, she triumphed over all of the challenges she faced during training, graduating with her friends as one of the top warriors. They marched off to face the Huns in battle soon after. During the events of the first battle, she came up with a plan to save them. She set off a rocket firework to start an avalanche which covered the Hun army and saved her friends. Unfortunately, she was badly wounded. In the tent where she was put to recover, her secret was found out. As a result, she was disgraced and discharged from the army. However, after discovering that the Huns had survived and were going to attack the capital city during the celebration of China's victory, she followed them to the city to warn the others. Her friends believed her and helped her to stop the attack and defeat the surviving Huns. The emperor found out that she was responsible for saving them and honored her by offering her a seat on the royal council. She declined, accepting the royal crest instead and returning home to her father. Through it all she overcame all of the trials she faced, becoming the first woman to join the army, fulfilling the destiny laid out before her and saving the nation.

LAUNCHED INTO DESTINY

Both of these stories show the progression that every story has from beginning to end. In the beginning of the stories the Pevensies and Mulan all experienced something that launched them into a journey of hardship, triumph and eventual destiny. The Pevensies' journey started with Lucy finding a magical world and a friend named Mr. Tumnus. She heard about the need that the Narnians had, and it motivated her to invite her siblings to come back with her to save Narnia. Mulan experienced a love for her father that pushed her to join the army to save him. For all of them, their stories after these experiences led them on journeys of hardship, dishonor, betrayal, and ultimately triumph and destiny.

For us as regular people this looks similar. God is inviting us into our own individual, unique stories of destiny. Just as the stories of the children in Chronicles of Narnia and Mulan began with an experience that pushed them to begin a journey that led to their destinies, our story begins with us experiencing God in a way that launches us into a journey with Him. This journey, while full of challenges, will also allow us to experience transformation and purpose. What God wants us to experience most of all is His love. His love is the source and foundation of our destiny. In the next chapter we will look at how God invites us to experience His love, launching us into a destiny built upon that love.

Chapter 5

Invited Into Love

God is inviting us into a story, a story that will ultimately end with us achieving the destiny He has for us as we journey with Him. However, there has to be a catalyst that motivates us to step into this story. For us to step into the story of our lives that ultimately leads to us achieving our destiny, we must first understand that we are invited to experience God in a way that will allow us to see Him for who He really is. This experience will motivate us to want to follow Him and will shape us into who we eventually become. God is inviting us to experience LOVE, a love that transforms us and launches us into the journey of our destiny. You might be wondering "why love?" That question is best answered by asking another question: "what is love?"

WHAT IS LOVE?

Our society tells us that love is a feeling. However, it's a feeling that changes depending on circumstances and emotions. For instance, we say that we love the beach. We love pizza. We love going on hikes or road tripping. We love our family and friends. We love our spouse. However, the kind of love our society proclaims and teaches is conditional. Our "love" for things or people can increase or decrease depending on our emotions and experiences. We can stop loving Papa John's pizza if we have a bad experience at a Papa John's store. We can stop loving the beach if the beach is polluted or overcrowded with people. We can stop loving hikes if we get poison ivy, get bit by a snake, or if we get badly hurt during a hike. We can stop loving our friends and family if they do something to hurt or disappoint us, if we stop spending time together, or if we realize that they aren't the greatest friends. We can even stop loving our spouse and get a divorce if they don't treat us right, if we "fall out of love," or if someone "better" comes along. The kind of love that we experience in the culture we live in today, especially in the Western world, is a love that is based on our emotional reactions to our experiences and circumstances. It isn't stable and it isn't faithful. This love isn't what God has designed us to experience in a life with Him.

The love that God is calling our names and inviting us into is a love that is perfect and can never fail. It is a love that allows us to experience truth and freedom. It is a love that will "cover a multitude of sin" (1 Peter 4:8, NKJV), a perfect love that "casts out fear" (1 John 4:18, NKJV). It is consistent, never changing based on feelings, and is always faithful no matter what happens.

God Himself is the very definition of love. The apostle John emphasizes this by saying in 1 John 4:8 that "God is love." Therefore, if we want to know what love is, we must experience God. When we experience God, we experience perfect love. In order to understand and know true love we must know God, developing a relationship with Him. As we develop that relationship, He reveals the depths of His love to us and helps us to understand and respond to it.

A DOCTRINE OF LOVE

An Emotional Experience

Before we can truly accept God's invitation into love there is something extremely important that we must understand. Experiencing God's love is an emotional experience that leads to transformation. This is an important element in a life with Christ that some Christians miss because it isn't frequently taught in many churches. A lot of times churches teach that we shouldn't trust our feelings. Instead, we need to only depend on Scripture and the doctrine of the church to make our decisions. While it is true that we do need to have more dependence on the truth of Scripture rather than emotions when making decisions, there is something else to consider. While having a structured doctrine that is founded on Scripture is extremely important and is essential to having a healthy faith, if we completely disregard our emotions in favor of just doctrine, we fail to consider that emotions are a part of God's design. Leaving out the part that emotion plays in our lives limits our understanding of how God designs us to respond to His love.

The truth is God has emotions as well. If He created us in His image, then our emotions are part of His image as well. The problem is sin has corrupted us to the point where our emotions rule us instead of us ruling them. This is why a lot of churches focus more on doctrine rather than emotional experiences. Those experiences can be corrupted by sin and we can be led astray and deceived by false teaching when our emotions are not led by the Holy Spirit.

Because there is the risk that what we feel will not be scripturally accurate, a lot of churches try to avoid relying on emotional experiences with God to negate the risk of being led astray. They rely more heavily on their knowledge of God rather than their emotional experiences with God.

However, only depending on our knowledge can limit how we respond to His love. God wants to redeem our emotions as part of the transformation process. He wants to teach us how to follow the Holy Spirit with our emotions so that we can use self-control and wisdom. Once our emotions are submitted to the Holy Spirit, we can experience God's love fully and respond to it appropriately. I will talk more about this in a later chapter.

Love is Felt

In establishing a healthy doctrine of love, we must understand that experiencing God's love has to start with our emotions. It has to be felt in order to be processed and understood. Let's look at our own experiences with natural love to explain this further. A father of a newborn baby experiences a deep emotion for his newborn son. This emotion that the father feels causes him to want to protect, to nurture, to hold, etc. his child. We call this emotion love. Another example is a bride and groom on their wedding day. The bride sees the groom standing at the front waiting for her, perhaps crying or smiling as he waits for her. In my case, my bride saw me standing there with a big grin on my face, tongue sticking out of my mouth, causing her to laugh AND cry at the same time as she came down the aisle! If you know us, you know that this is normal for how we express our emotions of love. We laugh, cry, and do weird things. Perhaps those of you reading also have a unique way of expressing love. It's perfectly natural. The emotion that we experience when we experience love is beyond what we can comprehend. It wells up and comes out in various expressions. It also pushes us to respond with an action of love as well. Love pushes a father to enjoy life with his son, protecting him, nurturing him, and helping him become the man he is supposed to be. Love pushes a bride and groom to make a covenant with each other on their wedding day, a covenant establishing a life of love, oneness, and faithfulness until death.

The same is true when we experience God's love with our emotions. As amazing as our human feelings of love are, our natural human love can't come close to what we experience when we encounter God's love for us. Some fall to their knees in worship when experiencing His love. Some start weeping. For all of us repentance is the ultimate response when we encounter His love. This experience brings the emotion of conviction by the Holy Spirit. When we encounter His love, we recognize in the deepest parts of our souls that we are sinners in need of Him. His love for us is indescribable and brings us to repentance. This conviction is an emotional as well as logical experience. We both know within our minds and feel within our hearts that we are sinners who are in need of a Savior. The response to this conviction is repentance that leads to transformation. This kind of love is what He is inviting us to experience within our emotions.

Love is...

Let's look at what the Bible says about love so we can see who God is and understand the love that He wants us to experience. Paul defines love perfectly in 1 Corinthians 13, also known as the "love chapter."

> "Love suffers long and is kind; love does not envy; love does not parade itself, is not puffed up; does not behave rudely, does not seek its own, is not provoked, thinks no evil; does not rejoice in iniquity, but rejoices in the truth; bears all things, believes all things, hopes all things, endures all things. Love never fails" (NKJV).

The love that God wants us to understand and experience in Him is a long-suffering kind of love. This means that no matter what happens that kind of love will still be there. It is patient. It is not demanding of its own way and isn't rude. If God is love, then that means God is patient and doesn't behave like a person demanding his or her own way, yelling and screaming, like some parents do when their child is misbehaving in Walmart. Thank God that He doesn't behave rudely by throwing a temper tantrum every time we mess up or He disagrees with what we are doing. Instead, He is gentle and never rude. No matter what we do, He still has a patient love for us. The Bible emphasizes this further in other scriptures. Exodus 34:6 describes God as being "slow to anger" (NASB) which means He has a lot of patience and can endure of lot of evil being done against Him before He gets angry.

Also, God's love is kind. You cannot have love without being both patient and kind. So many times, we hear the phrase "tough love" which is usually said by people who are trying to toughen their kids or friends up a little bit. While this kind of love might come from a good heart, oftentimes it is unnecessarily cruel and borderline abusive. It is quite possibly what Paul was correcting the Corinthians for doing, saying that love doesn't rejoice in iniquity. How many of you would respond well to a kind of love that rejoices in iniquity saying that it's "tough love?" I wouldn't. I'm sure most of you wouldn't either. Thankfully, the kind of love that God wants us to experience in Him isn't like that at all. He is kind and gentle. Some might see this kind of love as too soft, but I disagree. Saying that love is kind doesn't imply a love that doesn't correct and discipline. In fact, Paul says that it "rejoices in the truth" (1 Corinthians 13:6, NKJV). Truth partnered with love is patient, gentle, and kind but also brings transformation through correction and discipline. It is this kind of love that makes us want to change and "leads us to repentance" (Romans 2:4, NASB).

If God is love itself, then God Himself is kindness personified. He wants us to experience His kindness as He reveals the truth to us. However, there is something important to remember. Saying that God's love is kind doesn't imply that God's kindness will keep us from suffering. Suffering is a part of life because we live in a fallen world. On the other hand, God allowing suffering doesn't negate the fact that He is kind either. He is still good and full of love even though He allows evil. In fact, His plan for us is so good and perfect that He has put Himself in our shoes as a demonstration of His kind love for us and as an example to look to so that we can overcome the trials that we face. Jesus, God's Son, left His divinity to be born as a baby, enduring the same challenges of life that we face. He ultimately suffered more through His death on the cross than most of us ever will. In other words, God Himself suffered. This willingness to suffer extreme pain for us demonstrates His great love for us.

Also, the love that God embodies doesn't selfishly pursue and demand our devotion. Yes, He wants our devotion and attention. It's part of our covenant with Him when we declare that He is Lord of our lives. He is ours and we are His, just like a bride to her husband (Song of Songs 2:16). However, He doesn't force us to worship and obey Him. He lets us make our own choices to follow Him. We can choose to break that covenant with Him if we want to do our own thing. However, He is always faithful to restore our relationship with Him when we come back to Him.

Something that we should also never take for granted is that God's love is never puffed up or arrogant. Rather than being demanding and drawing attention to Himself, God always focuses more on others. This means that love should always focus more on others rather than oneself. This kind of love takes humility, putting others first, and is never envious when love is unaccepted or returned. He extends this love toward us, believing in us, enduring our disobedience and rebellion, bearing our burdens and pain, hopeful that we will respond to His love. This is the kind of love that God is inviting us to experience when we encounter Him. This is the kind of love that "leads to repentance" as I stated earlier. This is the kind of love that is worth following.

LOVE: THE BREEDING GROUND FOR DESTINY

When we encounter God, we experience a love that is patient and long-suffering in every situation, never demanding its own way, or parading itself. A love that corrects with the truth but is also gentle and kind. This true, lasting love, a love that can only come from a perfect God, is where our purpose is found. God's love is the fertile ground that we can be planted in and experience growth and transformation, the soil where our talents and abilities can grow.

His love is where we find out who we are through experiencing who He is. Only through encountering God's love can we achieve our destiny. God is inviting us by name into His love, calling us to experience who He is. He is inviting us to be planted in this love and experience growth and transformation. This love allows us to thrive in every area like He intends. How will you respond?

Chapter 6

Invited To Love God

Let's back up for a second. God wants us to experience His love. How do we experience God in order to know Him and better understand love? It's simple. I gave the answer to this in the first chapter. You seek Him with all of your heart. As I have been saying, He is already inviting us by name to experience Him, drawing us by his Holy Spirit. Having the faith to seek Him is how we respond to His invitation and the drawing of the Holy Spirit. When we find Him, He reveals His love to us. But there still must be a response to His love in order for there to be true lasting transformation. Just like our natural emotions of love motivate us to respond with acts of love, there has to be a response to the emotional experience that we have when we encounter His love.

Jesus tells us in Matthew 22:37 that the most important commandment given to us is to "Love the Lord your God with all your heart and with all your soul and with all your mind." This commandment is God's invitation for us to respond to His love in a way that He desires. He wants us to experience His love in a way that motivates us to love Him back with everything that we are.

Loving God isn't just an emotion though, there has to be action involved that demonstrates our love. That action is two-fold. Unless our hearts are hard, experiencing His love should always lead to us developing a love that is demonstrated through repentance. Repentance is having a mindset change about the sin in our lives, recognizing that we are sinful and need Him to change us. That recognition motivates us to turn away from our sin and towards Him in obedience to His commands. Just like a father protects his child in response to his love, repentance is our response to loving God. When we repent, we are submitting to His Lordship, declaring that He is Lord of our lives. We also demonstrate our love by continuing to pursue Him, developing a healthy, growing relationship with Him as Lord.

The Lordship of God

God is loving, kind, gentle, good, etc. These traits allow us to see that He is worthy of our love. However, we must never forget that He is also King of Kings and Lord of Lords. He is our Master and Leader. As His servants and subjects who follow Him, we must obey Him. He wouldn't be King of Kings and Lord of Lords if there was not a requirement to obey Him. If the kings and queens throughout history didn't require obedience to their rule while they were kings and queens, there would have been chaos. Rules that require obedience bring structure, justice, and peace to a society. The same can be said of God's rule over His kingdom. He is a just God, meaning that He is fair. His rules are beneficial and good for us but are also meant to prevent destruction. The Ten Commandments found in

Exodus are proof of His goodness and just nature. Each of these commands had a purpose. They were meant to keep the Israelites on His path for them instead of turning away to lesser gods. They were also meant to establish healthy rhythms of life by learning the value of rest. God instituted these commands as a way for them to be at peace and have unity with one another by preventing them from murdering, stealing, cheating, lying, etc. against one another. They are all practical commandments that will help them achieve their purpose in life. However, because He is just, the consequence of breaking these rules is His judgment. Because He cannot lie and go back on what He promises, He has to judge us when we disobey. We see His judgment of Israel throughout the Old Testament when they turned their backs on Him. However, we also see His mercy when they repented, showing His love for them.

That being said, He doesn't want our obedience out of just a fear of punishment. When we obey out of fear of punishment, we make our obedience more about ourselves than about Him. This is still the sin of pride. Instead, He wants our obedience to come from a place of love for Him because we don't want to hurt or grieve Him. Solomon says in Proverbs 9:10 that "the fear of the Lord is the beginning of wisdom" (NKJV). What this means is that we obey Him out of respect for who He is. We love our King and His commands. We love Him enough to put Him in a position of authority in our lives. Because we love Him, we want to respect His Lordship over our lives with our obedience, not grieving and dishonoring Him by disobeying. A life of wisdom begins with loving God, respecting His position of authority and lordship in our lives, and obeying His commands out of love and respect.

God Our Father

However, God doesn't want us to follow and obey Him just because He is Lord and commands us to. Yes, we might love Him as Lord, and that love for His lordship compels us to obey the laws He sets, as we see in Israel's relationship with Him. However, we also see that obedience to the law doesn't lead to true, lasting transformation. It requires a heart change that can only come from having a deep relationship with God. The Israelites kept turning away from God when their hearts got distracted by lesser gods. This was because they didn't know and love Him deeply in the way He wanted them to. Even following the law religiously distracted them from truly knowing God, as we see when the nation of Israel didn't recognize Jesus as God and crucified Him. This is an important principle to remember. Only a deep relationship with God and experiencing the fullness of who He is can truly change us. Only by fully knowing and experiencing Him can we truly love Him in a way that allows us to follow and obey Him without getting distracted by lesser things.

In understanding this principle, it is important to remember that God is not only our Lord. He is also our Father. Scripture affirms this when Paul tells us in Romans 8:14-17, "For as many as are led by the Spirit of God, these are sons of God. For you did not receive the spirit of bondage again to fear, but you received the Spirit of adoption by whom we cry out, 'Abba, Father.' The Spirit Himself bears witness with our spirit that we are children of God, and if children, then heirs, heirs of God and joint heirs with Christ, if indeed we suffer with Him, that we may also be glorified together" (NKJV). When we experience God's love for us and respond to it by loving Him back, we become

His sons and daughters, establishing a deeper relationship with Him than just as Lord.

Friend of God

Not only is He our Lord and Father, though. He is also our Friend. Jesus also tells those who follow Him in John 15:14-15 "you are My friends if you do whatever I command you. No longer do I call you servants, for a servant does not know what his master is doing; but I have called you friends, for all things that I heard from My Father I have made known to you" (NKJV).

When we understand this principle our relationship with Him immediately shifts to a different dynamic. Yes, He is still Lord, but now He is also Father and Friend. As His children, we have access to Him as His sons and daughters, with all the privileges as His heirs. As His friend we have an intimacy with Him that goes beyond the normal acquaintance. This implies a deeper relationship than just as a servant to a Lord. It's personal. It brings to life the fact that He doesn't just rule us from afar but is close. Not only that, but it also demonstrates His love for us. He loves us so much that He calls those who follow Him and are led by His Spirit His children and His friends.

The question that we have to ask ourselves, however, is do we feel the same way. Is He our friend that sticks closer than a brother? Is He our Father that we can run to in every situation? Or is He just someone we're afraid of, following His rules blindly out of Christian duty? How we respond to experiencing His love will reflect the answer to this question. Does experiencing His love make us want to deepen our relationship with Him, following Him and loving Him as our Lord, Father, and Friend, or do we respond by being afraid of Him, living our lives following a set of rules instead of getting to know Him as more than just Lord and Master?

OUR PURPOSE IS TO LOVE

Which category do you belong in? I know lots of people who were raised in churches that were more "legalistic" demanding perfection, but not really teaching about how to love God. However, we must remember that what God is inviting us into is not just about following a set of rules. It's about experiencing His love in a way that will push us to respond by loving Him back with everything that we are. He wants us to love Him as Lord, Father, and Friend. Our response to experiencing God's love will shape our relationship with Him and determine how far it will go.

As I have said all throughout the last few chapters, God is inviting us into a story. It's a story of experiencing His love and responding to it with love. It's a story of a journey filled with experiences that will transform us into stronger, more confident individuals who thrive in every area of life. This is the plan that God has for our lives. Only when we follow His design for our lives can we find our purpose and achieve the extraordinary destiny we have in Him.

So many of us ask "what is my purpose?" I'll go ahead and give you the answer now. Pay attention. Are you ready?

As part of our journey with God towards our destiny He is inviting us into love. Love is the central foundation of our purpose. In fact, our primary purpose in life is to first and foremost love Him with all of our being and then to love others as ourselves. Did you catch that? I'll repeat myself. Your primary purpose, the reason you were created, is to LOVE GOD WITH ALL YOUR HEART, SOUL,

MIND, AND STRENGTH and to LOVE PEOPLE AS YOURSELF.

Loving Him as Lord, Father, and Friend in response to experiencing His love is the first step into that purpose. Loving others as much as ourselves is the second step on the journey and is the result of experiencing His love and loving Him. Any other goals and plans that God has designed for us to accomplish during our lifetimes are secondary and are meant to help us fulfill these purposes. When we love Him and love others, we can then use our lives to help grow His kingdom. However, it all starts when we choose to respond to His love and choose to get to know Him more so that we can love Him more. Without this choice we cannot find our destiny.

Chapter 7

Invited To Know God

I n the last chapter I introduced this principle that is the foundation of this book: our primary purpose that we have been created to achieve is to love God. Loving God is the foundation of our relationship with Him. However, there is another factor that plays a huge part in how healthy our relationship with God will be. How do you maintain your love for God?

Asking the question "Do I know God, or do I know about God" will determine how you view God. Our knowledge and understanding of who God is plays a huge part in how we develop our relationship with Him. If our knowledge of Him is limited, then our relationship with Him will be limited. It's the same principle as how we maintain our natural relationships. If we don't put the effort into understanding and truly knowing the people who we confess to love, our relationship with them will be limited. A healthy, growing relationship of any form requires healthy communication that leads to better understanding of each other. It starts with love. Love pushes us to communicate in order to grow the relationship.

The same is true of our relationship with God. Our response to His love should be a deep love that pushes us to learn who He is by communicating directly with Him. If loving Him is our primary purpose, we can't just settle for knowing about Him. Scripture tells us that the demons know about Him and believe in Him, (James 2:19) but they obviously don't love Him or have a healthy relationship with Him. He isn't their Lord, Father, or Friend. In fact, He is their enemy.

GROWING IN LOVE

We need to ask ourselves this very important question: Do I know about Jesus, or do I know Him? The only way to answer this is to examine your lifestyle. What do you do to grow your relationship with Jesus? How much time do you spend with Him, learning who He is? We have to constantly be seeking Him directly to discover who He is. He provides us with several ways to do this: scripture, prayer, and community.

Scripture

Scripture is the primary method we have of discovering who God is and how He wants us to build a relationship with Him. The Bible is the story of God's love that He is inviting us to read in order to better know Him, and see Him as Lord, Father, and Friend. Reading the Bible will help us understand how to love Him with everything we are in response to experiencing His love. Through studying the Bible, we develop an understanding of God's character and how He wants to transform us as we respond to His invitation. However, studying scripture has to be approached in conjunction with prayer and community in order to gain the most out of it.

Prayer

Prayer is communication with God. Communication is a two-way process between two individuals, in this case us and God. When we pray, we are not only communicating to God through our prayers; He is communicating back to us. When we communicate with someone every day, that person becomes more than just an acquaintance. We learn who they are, and a relationship is formed. For the relationship to thrive, there must be consistent, intentional, healthy communication. Our relationship with God works the same way. When we declare Jesus as Lord, the Holy Spirit enters our lives and helps us to know and love Him. He teaches us to pray, reveals the truth of Scripture to us, helps us to understand it, and deepens our relationship with God, equipping and transforming us as we follow Him.

Through prayer, or communicating with God through the Holy Spirit, He reveals Himself to us and opens our eyes to the truth. Scripture comes alive at this moment when we talk to Him about it. As a result, we are forever changed. Our relationship with Him deepens as we continue to experience His presence and develop healthy communication habits with Him.

In order to establish a healthy relationship with God through the Holy Spirit, we must have consistent, healthy times of intentional communication with Him through prayer. When we practice this principle, we learn who He is and our relationship with Him deepens. As our desire for Him grows through prayer, our desire to read scripture and join with others who know Him in community grows as well.

Community

Community is the third way that we learn who God is and develop a relationship with Him. This method is extremely important because it allows us to experience Him in new ways through establishing healthy relationships with others who also know Him. Those of us who know and follow Jesus are part of a family made up of individuals who have all experienced God's invitation into love and responded to it in unique ways. We all have unique personalities, ways of understanding and interpreting scripture, and hearing from God. If we work together, we can all learn from one another how to love God more and how to grow our relationship with Him. I'll talk more about this in a later chapter. However, how much we grow in community, and ultimately, how much our relationship with God grows, is determined by one more important principle. God is inviting us to not only love Him with everything that we are but also to love others as much as ourselves.

LOVE GOD, LOVE PEOPLE

God is inviting us to experience His love in a way that will motivate us to love Him "with all your heart and with all your soul and with all your mind." (Matthew 22:37, NKVJ). However, this invitation doesn't stop there. Jesus continues telling us in the next verse that the second greatest commandment is to "love your neighbor as yourself." We see with this statement that God's invitation is not only to love Him; it is also an invitation for us to love others just as much as we love ourselves.

Unfortunately, as fallen humans who are self-focused because of pride, it is impossible to love others as much as we love ourselves. Fortunately, God has taken this weakness into account as He has planned His design for our lives. The answer is part of His invitation into His love. The love that He is inviting us to experience as we encounter Him transforms us and allows us to love others like He loves. I'll talk more about how God has designed us to love others in a later chapter.

Responding to His love by giving Him our love is just the beginning. His invitation into love is also an invitation to join Him on a journey as His disciple. This journey begins with love, is filled with transformation and purpose as we respond by giving our lives, and results in us achieving the destiny God has for us. Over the next few chapters I will be discussing what happens when we respond to His invitation into love as we journey with Him as His disciple.

Part 2 Discipleship

"Then He said to them, 'Follow Me'"

Matthew 4:19

Chapter 8

Invited Into Discipleship

A few years ago, I went through a season where I had to let go of my dreams in order to figure out what God's purpose for my life was. This season started when I had to step down from a ministry position that had become my life, giving up a dream that I thought God had called me to. The disappointment and hurt that I felt in this moment led me into a three-year season of searching as I tried to replace the dream that I had lost with a new one. During this three years God placed me in a position at a church serving as young adult's pastor. I knew this was where God had called me, but I also knew that it was temporary and that I needed to find out what God was doing in my life. As a result, even though I was serving God as the young adult's pastor, I wasn't serving Him as well as I could have, constantly distracted trying to figure out my future. I experienced severe discontentment that led to me making choices that weren't the best for me or part of God's plan. Instead of simply serving and being content with what God was doing where I was, I looked too much to the future, to my next ministry assignment. I kept asking God what His plan was and grew more and more frustrated when He didn't give me a specific answer. I made choices and plans out of desperation trying to get God to confirm that I was making the right choices. However, these decisions were never God's will and I never felt peace about them. I prayed and fasted trying to figure out what I was supposed to do with my life, but never got an answer. This lasted almost three years until one day I realized that I was trying too hard and had lost who I was. I wasn't growing and had become more and more frustrated and disillusioned in every aspect of my life because of my situation. I immediately realized that I had reached the breaking point and I needed to stop what I was doing or I would fall into depression. God spoke to me something that has stuck with me since then. He said "life with Me isn't a run to chase what I have for you, it's a walk beside me." I realized immediately that I was running and chasing things that I thought were Him, when He just wanted me to walk with Him. I needed to stop and let go of everything I was trying to do. God spoke to me in this moment and told me that if I let go of the identity that I thought I had as a pastor, as well as the dreams that I had to do great things in His name, and simply follow Him as His disciple, He would use me as He wanted. I immediately felt a huge peace about what I had to do. I had to let go of the things that I knew weren't what He wanted me to do. I resigned from my role as young adults pastor and spent the next few months learning how to rest. It was in this moment that God started me on a journey to teach me what it truly means to be His disciple.

After hearing this story, you might be asking "but you've served Jesus your entire life, right? Weren't you already His disciple?" My answer is yes, I have served Jesus my entire life and yes, I have always been His disciple. Understand this, though. Although we are all Jesus's disciples, we are all on a journey at various stages of learning. Some learn more quickly than others, some learn less quickly. I wish that I had learned what God wanted to show me without having to go through the season of discontentment that I went through that almost led to burnout. If I had learned it beforehand I probably wouldn't have had to go through this season. But I had to in order to let go of my own plans and learn what God's plan for me actually was. Others learn this lesson too late, experiencing moral failure in some form and leaving their relationship with Jesus.

From my experience as well as seeing many others go through similar experiences, I would say that we have developed a bad understanding of what it truly means to follow Jesus in every area of life. There are a lot of people who are stuck in the same way I was even if they've served Him twice as long as me. Most of them don't even realize that they are stuck because they think they are in God's will, when they're actually not. There's a reason why so many pastors are leaving ministry. There's a reason why so many people only come to church to fulfill their religious duty. There's a reason why so many people don't understand their purpose in life and are anxious, worried all of the time, fearful, depressed, etc. It's because we don't know how to follow Jesus the way He designed us to. That might sound harsh, but the reality is, I know a lot of people who have had the same experience as I had, but didn't learn what God was teaching them. Most are stuck where they are in life.

I believe that there is more that God wants to teach those of us in western culture about following Him than we realize, especially in the season we're in as a culture. There are so many "truths" that society proclaims and doctrines that even churches teach that aren't scripturally accurate. I believe that God is calling His church into a new era of growth where He wants to teach us what it truly means to follow Him. That's what the purpose of this book is. God wants to help us discover our purpose as His disciples so that those who are a part of the church, no matter how young or old, can understand their destiny. When we learn to follow Jesus the way He designed us to, we can learn to thrive in every area of life as we experience His love that transforms us to be like Him.

A LOVE THAT TRANSFORMS

God is calling us into a story of love that will lead us to our destiny. The purpose that He has for us is perfect and will allow us to experience transformation and freedom, eternal reward, and a supernatural life. He calls us out by name, inviting us to experience His transformational love and step into a life with Him. Responding to this experience by confessing Him as Lord launches us into a journey with Him as His disciples. It is a journey that is filled with transformation, growth, and freedom as we learn what it means to love Him with our whole lives as Lord, Father, and Friend and how to love others as ourselves. This journey is a process, though. This process is what we call discipleship, the process of learning what it means to be His followers and how to love Him and love others well. There are steps in this process that we must understand to fully fulfill the purpose of loving Him and loving others that He has given us. Over the course of the following chapters I want to look at this process so that we can have a clear picture of what happens on the journey to achieving our destiny. First, lets talk about what discipleship actually is.

WHAT IS DISCIPLESHIP?

Jesus is inviting us to be His disciples. We become His disciples in response to experiencing His love. What does it mean to be His disciple, though? Today we describe this as "following Jesus" and "having a relationship with Him." While this is true, I don't think this entirely illustrates what being a disciple of Jesus means. Whenever I hear the phrase "relationship with Jesus," I think of a friendship or a romantic relationship. However, He's more than that to me. Yes, He is my Friend. But He is also my Lord. He is my Savior. We must learn to love God as Lord, Father, and Friend. To love Him in this way we must learn what it means to be Jesus's disciple.

In Scripture, when Jesus called His disciples, He didn't just call them to follow Him around or to just be friends with Him. He called them to learn from Him and emulate Him. In fact, the word "disciple" has a deeper meaning in the original language. It comes from the Greek word *matheteuo*. We use the word "follower" to translate it, but it actually is better translated as the word "pupil."[1] Another word that would also be fitting is "apprentice."

To give this concept a little more historical context, let's look at the Jewish culture back in Jesus's time. At this point in their history, Jewish rabbis were the most educated people around. They knew the law extremely well, memorizing it and learning about it from the time they could understand. Rabbis would take pupils who would study under them. They would look for specific talents and traits that would fit the type of student they were looking for. They would spend years mentoring and training these students to take their places as teachers of the law. Paul, for instance, was the disciple or pupil of

Gamaliel, a very prestigious Pharisee before he became a follower of Jesus.

To give other illustrations of what a student or apprentice is, let's look at other historical cultures. In the Middle Ages before the college and university systems were created, young teenagers would "apprentice" with master craftsmen to learn whatever trade they wanted to go into, usually the same as their fathers. Blacksmiths and other masters would search for apprentices who would learn from them and eventually go out and start their own businesses. They had to have the traits and skills necessary to be their apprentices, though.

In modern times, this is the same equivalent as going to trade school or university to develop a specific set of skills to pursue a specific career. Students learn from master teachers or professors until they are ready to start their own practice or work in their fields of study. Most college degrees demonstrate that the student has become an expert in their field when they are given a degree. People who want to advance further in their field can get a master's or doctoral degree demonstrating a more advanced expertise in their field. These students spend years studying to become experts in their field.

This is what Jesus was doing when He called His disciples. As a rabbi, He was choosing His "pupils" or "apprentices" who would follow Him and learn how to be like Him in every way. Unlike other rabbis at that time, though, He chose men and women who were considered the lowest in society to be His disciples, showing that He doesn't show partiality or favoritism as Scripture says in Romans 2:11. When it was time, He sent them out to be His ambassadors and grow His kingdom.

He does the same thing with us today. He invites us to

become His students. Something to note about this invitation is that it is a lifelong commitment to study under Jesus as His pupils. Discipleship isn't something to take lightly. Unfortunately, it is hard to love Jesus the way He wants by becoming His disciples. In fact, it's impossible. We need His help to do it. This is the story of the gospel.

Chapter 9

Discipleship: The Story Of The Gospel

God is inviting us to become Jesus's disciples so that we can learn how to accomplish our primary purpose: loving Him with all of our being. However, the truth is this: before we become followers of Jesus, we are slaves to our own sin nature. We love ourselves more than we love anything else. The cost of discipleship is that we give up everything to follow Him. Jesus emphasizes this principle in Matthew 16 when He states that the cost of following Him is taking up our cross, implying that we must die to ourselves if we are to follow Him. Unfortunately, we can't possibly love Him enough to lay down our lives for Him and take up our cross. We are way too self centered. We didn't start out that way, though.

The beginning of the story of God's love that He invites us into was this: God's intentions for mankind were perfect. We were to be perfect in nature just as much as He was, representations of Him on the earth, bearing His image to all of creation. God created Adam and Eve in His image, perfect and pure. They were the ultimate creation, the ones into whom God had breathed His breath, the very essence of who He is, giving them life. He gave them authority over all the earth, telling them to take dominion over it. However, they gave up this authority to Satan when they disobeyed God's command to not eat the forbidden fruit causing sin to enter creation.

Because sin cannot exist in the presence of God, the consequence of their choice was mankind's eternal separation from God and death. They were cursed, forced to leave the garden of Eden to wander the earth, enduring hardships that were never God's design for them. However, God had a plan. A plan that would demonstrate His grace and mercy and make it so mankind could come back into a relationship with Him and gain freedom from sin and death.

Throughout the rest of the book of Genesis we see sin didn't completely keep mankind from experiencing relationship with God. There were those who, in spite of their sinful nature, remained righteous and had a relationship with God. Noah, one of these men, was spared from the destruction of the earth by the flood along with his family. Abram, who later became Abraham, was a friend of God and who we know as the father of what would become the Christian faith. Jacob became known as Israel, or prince of God because of his relationship with God and faith in Him. He was the father of the nation of Israel, God's chosen people. Because of their relationship with God, each of these men played a huge role in the story of redemption that progressed from that point in the Bible.

Fast forward a few hundred years, further into the story, and we see God establish a covenant with His chosen people, Israel. He gave them the law that we see in Leviticus and Deuteronomy, establishing a system that would allow them to atone for their sins each year. A sacrifice would be made of an animal, usually a pure, spotless lamb, to take on the sins of the entire nation for the year. This animal would take their punishment for them. While this worked to reestablish a relationship with God to some extent, it could not completely redeem mankind for all eternity. We were still separated from God and couldn't know Him fully. God knew this, though. He had a plan that included the answer. Humanity needed some help from God Himself. The law was meant to show us that. Fulfilling the law required a pure spotless sacrifice. Only He was perfect enough to be the pure, spotless sacrifice that would completely atone for the punishment we deserved because of sin. Only He was capable of transforming hearts that are so easily led astray and corrupted.

A few hundred years after Israel's captivity in Babylon, and their eventual return, we see something happen that would change things forever: God Himself became a man in the form of Jesus, lived a perfect life, and then died in order to fulfill every requirement for our eternal redemption. We didn't have to do a thing. He did it for us.

That wasn't the end, though. He came back to life after three days, demonstrating His power over death. Because of this, not only is our debt of eternal punishment paid for, but we can have freedom from sin and the hope of eternal life with Him when we declare Him as Lord of our lives. This is the truth of the gospel that we discover when we accept His invitation to be His disciples. As we enter into this relationship, the Holy Spirit enters into our life, helping us to become the disciples He has designed us to be. This begins our partnership with Him as His disciples that allows us to find and fulfill our purpose of loving Him with all of our beings and loving others as ourselves. Accepting His invitation into love begins the discipleship process.

A LIFELONG COMMITMENT

I mentioned in an earlier chapter that God's calling is personal. The word "called" that is used throughout the New Testament is the Greek word *kaleō* which means "to invite" and" to call out by name."[1] So, when God calls us to follow Him, He is calling us out by name, inviting us to be His "apprentices." We are invited into discipleship for life. The question is, how will we respond to the invitation? If we do respond, how much of our lives are we giving to Him? How we respond demonstrates how much love we have for Him and how willing we are to seek out the purpose He has for us.

Jesus describes the Kingdom of Heaven and the calling to follow Him as a wedding feast in Matthew 22:1-14.

> "And Jesus answered and spoke to them again by parables and said: 'The kingdom of heaven is like a certain king who arranged a marriage for his son and sent out his servants to call those who were invited to the wedding; and they were not willing to come. Again, he sent out other servants, saying, 'Tell those who are invited, " 'See, I have prepared my dinner; my oxen and fatted cattle are killed, and all things are ready. Come to the wedding.'" But they made light of it and went their ways, one to his own farm, another to his business. And the rest seized his servants, treated them spitefully, and killed them. But when the king heard about it, he was furious. And he sent out his armies, destroyed those murderers, and burned up their city. Then he said to his servants, "'The wedding is ready, but those who were invited were not worthy. Therefore, go into the highways, and as many as you find, invite to the wedding.'" So those servants went

out into the highways and gathered together all whom they found, both bad and good. And the wedding hall was filled with guests. But when the king came in to see the guests, he saw a man there who did not have on a wedding garment. So, he said to him, "

'Friend, how did you come in here without a wedding garment?'" And he was speechless. Then the king said to the servants, "'Bind him hand and foot, take him away, and cast him into outer darkness; there will be weeping and gnashing of teeth. For many are called, but few are chosen'" (NKJV).

As this parable illustrates, the calling to follow Jesus is not an invitation to ignore or to take lightly. While all are invited to be His disciples, we can still make the choice to come halfheartedly. Discipleship requires all of our lives. There is a cost to following Jesus and we cannot take it lightly, as the people did who came to the wedding without proper attire. We must be prepared to do whatever God requires us to. Jesus tells us that to follow Him means sacrificing ourselves and giving up everything for the sake of the gospel. He puts it pretty bluntly in Matthew 16:24-26:

> "Then Jesus told his disciples, 'If anyone would come after me, let him deny himself and take up his cross and follow me. For whoever would save his life will lose it, but whoever loses his life for my sake will find it. For what will it profit a man if he gains the whole world and forfeits his soul? Or what shall a man give in return for his soul?'" (NKJV).

This might seem scary to some. The cost of following Jesus might seem too much to give. It might even seem ridiculous to some. Who would want to give up their lives for something? However, we must understand something about the cost of discipleship. We might give up a lot, but what we get in return for accepting His invitation and giving up everything to follow Him is priceless. When we give Him our lives and our love, we gain a greater treasure in Him. He gives us truth and freedom. He gives us hope for a better future, a destiny filled with "joy unspeakable and full of glory" (1 Peter 1:8, KJV).

Some might reject Him because they don't want to give up the good life they have. We must realize that while our lives might be good on the earth, what awaits us in hell isn't worth experiencing a good life without Him. But, when we accept His invitation to love Him with all of our hearts as His disciples, He gives us a way out of that eternal torment, saving us with His gift of grace and love. When we accept this gift and become His disciples, we will experience trials on earth, but we will also experience the life that He wants us to live. This life filled with His love will extend way past our last moments in life and will last for all eternity.

The hope of salvation and eternal destiny we have in Him is worth the cost. Everything else is a shadow that will fade away. He is extending an invitation of grace and mercy to us when He invites us to follow Him. The thing about His grace and love, though, is that it has to be received for it to take effect. We have the choice whether to take the freedom that He wants to give us or to reject it in favor of doing our own thing. In order to attend the "wedding feast" we must put off the clothes that we had before and put on the appropriate wedding clothes that He gives us. Living a life of freedom requires us to die to the old ways of doing things. Yes, it's hard. We will face trials and have to endure pain during the seasons God leads us through. However, what we gain as we become who God wants us to be is worth the pain. We must accept His invitation to follow Him, dying to ourselves as we go through the growth process.

I mentioned in a previous chapter that the emotion of our love should always motivate us to respond with an action of love that leads us to repentance. Becoming Jesus's disciple is that action. We must respond to experiencing His love by accepting His invitation to follow Him, becoming His disciples in every area of life. This is how we love God with everything that we are, fulfilling the first part of His purpose for our lives.

Chapter 10

Discipleship: His Creative Power

L et me reiterate this principle of discipleship in another way: God's invitation into discipleship is an invitation for us to experience His creative power within us, helping us to love Him with all of our beings as His disciples.

Jesus came to bring mankind out of captivity to sin and death, into freedom and new life. This is the story that God is inviting every man and woman into: leaving the old life behind and beginning a new life with Christ. I'll talk more about this new life in one of the next chapters. The only way for us to be whole and complete like God wants, is if we accept this truth and follow Him. This is what I want every one of you to get out of this book. If any of you are searching for purpose and truth, this is it. There are many "truths" out there for us to believe in and follow in order to find God, go to heaven, better ourselves, to achieve enlightenment and perfection, but they all eventually lead to self-destruction. There is one truth that stands above them all and it's this: Jesus is "the way, truth, and life" (John 14:6). This truth has stood the test of time and is the hope for all mankind. Through this truth, we can be like Jesus and find true wholeness, peace, joy, love, and eventual perfection. All we have to do is accept the invitation to experience His love in a way that transforms us. However, until we see and accept this truth and experience His love, we are doomed to stay slaves to sin.

The heart of God is this: He wants to bring all men out of darkness into His marvelous light (1 Peter 2:9). We who are separated from Him by sin need Him to bring us back into relationship with Him. The only way to do this is if this truth is revealed to us. Before this revelation, we are in darkness, blinded by the lies that we believe about ourselves and the world we live in. We need Him to open up our eyes. A better way to say it is that we need Him to give us new eyes to see His purpose for our lives clearly.

GIVEN NEW SIGHT

In the natural, God created our eyes with the ability to see by the means of light bouncing off whatever image is in front of you and then coming into your eyes. Our brains then process this light so that we perceive the shape and color of the image we're "seeing." Blindness is the inability to perceive the light bouncing off the image. So, when Jesus healed the blind man by spitting in mud and rubbing it into his eyes in John 9, He was recreating the missing pieces his eyes needed to be able to perceive the light.

Our ability to hear works much the same way. Sound waves enter the outer ear and pass through different inner parts of the ear, causing them to vibrate. Our brains then interpret these vibrations as sounds. Deafness is caused when the pieces that vibrate are missing or are broken and can't react to the sound waves.

Spiritually, we are so far from the light of Christ that we live as though we are blind and deaf. We do not have the ability to perceive the light of Christ or hear the truth that the Holy Spirit is whispering to our hearts. There are pieces of our lives that are broken and missing. We need Him to be those missing pieces, recreating what is broken within us. We need Him to open our eyes and give us new sight, just as Jesus did with the blind man, so that we can see Him clearly. We need Him to open our ears to hear His voice. Fortunately, He is up to the task of creating those missing pieces in every part of us.

God is our creator. He is Lord. We see in Genesis that God created the heavens and the earth. We also see Jesus opening the blind eyes and the deaf ears, as I've mentioned. He is a God of miracles. He not only creates physical things but spiritual things as well that will allow us to hear His voice and perceive the light of truth. David illustrates this in Psalm 51:10. "Create in me a clean heart, O God, and renew a steadfast spirit within me" (NKJV).

Notice, though, that David had a heart open to this creation. He asked for it because he recognized his need for a clean heart. This was right after he sinned with Bathsheba. He understood that he had messed up and needed God to step in to recreate what was broken and missing. He understood the call to repentance.

Invited into Repentance

In order for this creative power to work and for new life to be created inside of us, we have to be open to it. Before salvation, our hearts must be soft. We must recognize our need for a savior who can create a clean heart within us. Before we are saved, the Holy Spirit is calling, inviting us to experience His love, and inviting us to recognize our need for a savior and to repent. John 16:8 says, "And when He has come, He will convict the world of sin, and of righteousness, and of judgment" (NKJV).

The word "convict" here is the Greek word *elegchō* which means "to bring to light, to expose, to correct."[1] When something is brought to light or exposed, it implies that it was once hidden from our sight. To put it in scientific terms, just like the light has to bounce off an object and hit our eyes in order for us to see it, the truth has to be illuminated to us by the light of the Holy Spirit and brought to our spiritual eyes. Before our eyes are opened, we are blind to the truth because the light of truth either hadn't "bounced" yet into our eyes, or hadn't been revealed to us at that point, or we couldn't perceive that light even it had been revealed because of sin blinding us. As the Holy Spirit calls out to us by name, inviting us to follow Jesus and step into the new life He has for us, He brings to light or reveals our sin. He also reveals the standard of righteousness that God wants us to have through the example of Jesus, and the judgment that we will face if we do not accept this invitation, choosing to remain in darkness.

As the Holy Spirit calls and invites us to follow Jesus, we have a choice. We can choose to allow our eyes and ears to be opened by Him as we recognize our need for Him as He convicts us of our sin, or we can harden our hearts, staying blind and deaf to the truth that He wants to reveal to us. If we choose to allow our eyes to be opened, the next step is to respond to His invitation to repent. Repentance is the key to transformation. Coming from the Greek word *metanoia*, which means "to have a change of mind,"[2] repentance implies that we change our behavior because our mind have been changed about that behavior. Once our eyes are open to sin as the Holy Spirit convicts and reveals that sin, our response should be to repent and allow Him to help us change our behavior. If we change our minds about sin and learn to hate it because of our love for God, we can then turn away from it and behave in obedience to God's commands.

Invited to Heart Change

However, we can't change on our own. We need the help of the Holy Spirit to continue to change our hearts. Behavior overflows from the heart. Our hearts need to encounter the love of God so that we can respond with love, repentance, and obedience as His disciples. Notice David's response to his sin in Psalm 51:10 that I mentioned before. "Create in me a clean heart, O God, and renew a steadfast spirit within me." David recognized that he had done wrong. He also changed his mind about this sin and didn't want to do it again. Something else to understand, too, is that he also recognized that this was a part of him that needed to be transformed, and he couldn't do it without God's help. His heart had to be changed so that He could love God in a way that resulted in complete obedience. In order for His heart to be changed so that he could walk in obedience to God's commands, he had to put his relationship with God as his top priority. We see this all throughout the book of Psalms. God Himself had to be the center of His life. This priority shift would result in David getting a clean heart and right spirit within him. He had to grow in love for God and His commands in order to gain a new heart.

This process of transformation is the foundation of discipleship. In this process God creates new eyesight and a new heart so that we can see our need clearly and learn to love and obey Him. Once we see the truth and allow our hearts to respond to God's love by repenting, we can then pursue a relationship with Him as His disciples. As His disciples we learn to love Him as Lord, Father, and Friend and can continue in our journey of becoming like Him. This is also how we achieve our purpose of loving Him with all of our being and loving others as much as we love ourselves.

Chapter 11

Discipleship: The Invitation Into More

God has created each of us to be His followers. As we accept His invitation to follow Him and learn to love Him with every part of our being, He wants to give us everything that we need to become like Him in every way. He wants to give us the tools that will allow us to accomplish the purpose that we were created for. Not only that but He's willing to give us more than we could ever hope or ask for. He is a God of more than enough and He loves to give His children good gifts. His invitation into discipleship is also an invitation into more than just enough. It is an invitation into a life overflowing with His presence, His goodness, His peace, His grace, His love, joy, patience, etc. This is His plan for our lives. It is a plan that allows us to experience His love that helps us thrive in every area of our lives.

INVITED INTO HIS PRESENCE

It's important to remember that as God's disciples we have access to His presence. It's in His presence that we experience His love and learn to love Him. How many of us get the opportunity to be in the presence of kings, presidents, celebrities, etc. once in our lifetime? Barely any of us, unless we're lucky. It rarely happens. However, as disciples of Jesus, we get this privilege on a day-to-day basis. Accepting an invitation to become Jesus' disciples means that we are also accepting His invitation into His presence. We are walking in the presence of the King of Kings and Lord of Lords! How mind-blowing is that! We can be in the presence of our creator, savior, healer, and giver of everything we need!

That thought alone is enough to bring me to my knees in worship. Before Jesus's death we could not approach God because of our sin and separation from Him. When He died, however, the veil in the temple that separated the courtyard from the Holy of Holies was torn. This symbolized that the separation between God and humanity was gone. We now have unlimited access to the throne room of God. Even better, He is now living inside of us because when we accept His invitation to discipleship, we are also extending an invitation for Him to live inside of us. Paul tells us in 1 Corinthians 6:19 that our bodies are the temple of the Holy Spirit. We have 24/7 access into His presence that gives us everything that we need to find our purpose and accomplish our destiny. Paul emphasizes this in Hebrews 4:16. "Let us therefore come boldly to the throne of grace, that we may obtain mercy and find grace to help in time of need."

Only in His presence can we find the things that we need to be the people He has called us to be and become like Him. What do you need to find contentment and healing? Only His presence. Nothing else matters. In His presence there is freedom (2 Corinthians 3:17). In His presence, there is fullness of joy (Psalm 16:11). It's only through His presence where you will find healing. It's in His presence that you will find strength. Only in His presence will you find the grace and mercy you need to overcome shame and guilt. Only in His presence will you find comfort and peace to overcome anxiety and stress. Only in His presence can you experience this love that I have been talking about since the beginning of this book. Only in His presence can you fulfill the purpose of loving Him with everything you are and loving others as much as yourself. Only in His presence can you walk as His disciples. Discipleship is a lifelong commitment to walking in His presence beside Him.

Practicing Praise and Prayer

Let me ask this question again. What do you need? The answer is found by approaching Him and getting in His presence. Some of you might be saying, "But God seems so far off," "I'm not worthy to enter His presence," or "I can't feel His presence anymore." Let me ask you this question then if this describes your mindset. Are you praising Him? David says in Psalm 22:3 that God "inhabits the praises of His people." Another translation says that He is "enthroned on the praises of His people." This means that God comes into the room when we praise Him.

Another question we need to be asking ourselves if we don't feel God's presence is this: are we asking Him to come? God is faithful to respond to our invitation. In fact, He is already there by our side, but His presence is hidden from us until we acknowledge Him through praise.

Praise and prayer are important parts of the discipleship process and are useful practices that help us to build habits of staying in the presence of God. Praise puts Him in a position of authority and honor in our lives and prayer gives Him permission to move on our behalf. When we praise and ask for Him to reveal Himself, He responds by coming and showing us His glory and love. However, we can easily become distracted from His presence if we don't train our minds and hearts to continually respond to His invitation to be in His presence. Because we are human, it's our job to develop the habit and mindset of remaining in His presence just as He remains with us. I'll talk about this more in a later chapter. Practicing the disciplines of praise and prayer helps us to always focus on Him throughout our journeys as His disciples. It also helps us to learn to love Him more as His disciples. When we focus our attention on Him and His presence, He brings transformation.

INVITED INTO FAITH

The invitation into discipleship also requires us to have the faith we need to take steps into the unknown. Here's the thing that a lot of followers of Jesus have forgotten: Jesus was not only a perfect man, He was also a man of action. He healed the sick, raised the dead, turned water into wine, walked on water, and cast out demons, demonstrating His love for people. His desire is for us to do the same things He did, and more. All it takes is for us to have the faith to obey. He wants us to be people of action who live out the gospel in faith and see Him move in the way He wants to. Yes, there will be times when He invites us into things that we don't understand. But, because we have experienced His love for us and have responded by becoming His disciples, we can trust that that love will never let us down.

The story of Peter walking on water in Matthew 14:22-33 has two lessons we can learn from. The first is that our focus determines our reality. If our focus is on Jesus, we will be like Him even through the storms. The second is this: Peter was the only disciple out of the twelve who had the faith to get out of the boat. The others just assumed they couldn't do it. How many of us never even think to step out in faith just because we assume we can't do what Jesus does? The reality is in today's culture most of us wouldn't even think about getting out of the boat.

I want to make this challenge for all of us as followers of Jesus. Our mentality about our potential as disciples of Jesus has to align with Scripture. This is the seed that God wants to plant inside of us. God has a destiny for us and a plan that is beyond our comprehension. Part of this plan is for us to live a supernatural lifestyle. Paul tells us in Philippians 4:13 that we can do all things "through Christ who strengthens us" (NKJV). Jesus Himself tells us that we will do all that He did and even greater things if we follow Him (John 14:12). If He tells us to do something, we can do it. That is His promise to us. Paul emphasizes this in 2 Timothy 3:16-17 saying, "all Scripture is given by inspiration of God, and is profitable for doctrine, for reproof, for correction, for instruction in righteousness, that the man of God may be complete, thoroughly equipped for every good work" (NKJV). Paul was telling Timothy here that we are equipped with everything we need to grow the Kingdom, just like Jesus.

It is also important to remember that we don't have to do it in our own power. We don't have the capability of being His disciples and living a supernatural life apart from Him. He does the work while we are His obedient followers. We don't save people, He does. We don't heal, He does. All we have to do is just take the step out of the boat with Him when He tells us to and follow Him out onto the water. He will lead us with His Spirit, giving us the words to say, and telling us what to do as He enables us to do it.

So, how do we become people of faith who can get out of the boat when Jesus calls? The answer to this is twofold: know God and know yourself. The two biggest reasons why we don't become who God has made us to be is that we either don't know God or haven't figured out or accepted our identity as His children. I'll talk more about our identity in a later chapter, but what I want to leave you with in this chapter is this: You can live the extraordinary life that God wants you to live. All it takes is accepting His invitation and responding to His love by becoming His disciple. The enemy, however, wants to steal this truth from us so that it can't be planted firmly inside of the good soil of our hearts. He wants to keep us from doing whatever it takes to grow ourselves and the Kingdom of God. He wants to keep us from surrendering our lives completely to Him as His disciples who love Him with all of our being and who love others as ourselves. However, the God who lives inside of you is stronger than the enemy and is inviting you to partner with Him to achieve His purpose and destiny for your life. He can give you the life that you need to live for Him every day, resisting the enemy, and loving Him in all that you do.

Chapter 12

Discipleship: New Life

G od has a destiny for each of us. The process of achieving that destiny, however, requires that we surrender our lives to a plan that is greater than ourselves. This process is called discipleship. Jesus is extending an invitation to us to become His disciples. As His disciples we learn to love Him with all we are and love others as much as we love ourselves. This will allow us to experience a destiny in Him that is beyond any destiny this world has to offer, a destiny so great it will produce eternal results. This journey towards destiny first starts when we experience His love that "leads us to repentance" (Romans 2:4, NKJV). Experiencing this love will open our eyes to the truth that we need a Savior who will bring us back into a relationship with God. This Savior is Jesus.

We have been invited into the story of His love. The message of the gospel story that we have been invited into is this: God created us in His image, perfect and good. But when sin entered the world through Adam and Eve's disobedience, His image inside of us was corrupted and we became self-focused. However, God had a plan of redemption. He sent Jesus into the world to die, fulfilling all requirements set by the law given by God to the people of Israel. Jesus died but then rose on the third day, victorious over death and sin.

We are part of this story. Discipleship is part of God's plan of redemption. Jesus is inviting us to experience His love and accept His invitation to be His disciples. Accepting this invitation will help us to fulfill our main purpose of loving Him with everything that we are and loving others as much as ourselves.

The question is, will we respond to the invitation? If we do respond, how much of our lives are we giving to Him? Discipleship requires us to die completely to ourselves, letting go of opinions and former ways of thinking and acting in order to truly understand the plans He has for us. It requires repentance or in the original language of the New Testament, the Greek word *metanoia*, which means to have a change of mind that leads to a behavior change. It also requires complete reliance on Him to help us to change our minds and behaviors. His love is what brings this transformation. We are to respond to His love by giving ourselves to Him as His disciples who love Him completely.

Once our eyes have been opened to the truth and we have repented, the Bible says in 2 Corinthians 5:17 that we have become a "new creation." At that moment, we step into a journey of discipleship and transformation that leads us to finding a supernatural eternal destiny of wholeness in every area. However, there is more we must understand about this verse. The full verse of 2 Corinthians 5:17 reads "Therefore, if anyone is in Christ, he is a new creation; old things have passed away; behold, all things have become new." We see here that we have to be in Christ in order to be a new creation. This means we have to accept His invitation to experience His love and then respond to it by becoming His disciples.

When we become Christ's disciples, we have to understand that the previous ways of doing things are now dead. When we declare Him as Lord of our lives and accept His invitation to be His disciple, we now have been given new life in Him and a new chance to love God with all of our being. It all starts when we respond to His love through repentance. We are completely 100% new creations. This means that we have to fill our lives with Him so that we don't revert back to the old ways of doing things. This is the process of sanctification and is a major part of the discipleship process. This process will ultimately bring transformation and allow us to achieve the purpose God designed us for; to love Him and love others well as His disciples. I want to focus on one important detail in this chapter that is extremely important to remember as we journey as His disciples: repentance leads to new life.

REPENTANCE THAT LEADS TO NEW LIFE

Repentance is the result of the Holy Spirit's conviction and is crucial in the transformation process. To put it simply, we cannot be Jesus's disciples without repentance because it is the foundation of discipleship and transformation. It begins with our hearts encountering His love in a way that shakes us to the core and makes us realize our need for Him. Repentance is our heart's response to this experience; a response that results in our mindsets shifting towards holiness and righteousness instead of sin and leads to transformation and new life.

Paul tells us in 2 Corinthians 5:17 "Therefore, if anyone is in Christ, he is a new creation; old things have passed away; behold, all things have become new" (NKJV). This shows us that when someone becomes a disciple of Jesus through repentance, they are made into new creations. They have been given new life.

Take for instance two testimonies of Jesus's saving grace. One individual, a drug addict, alone in life with no friends and family to care for him. The other, a college student who grew up in the church, but never experienced Jesus in a way that led to true transformation. Both encounter Jesus for the first time, experiencing the truth of His love and presence in a way that causes them to instantly give their lives to Him. They both have been cleansed of their pasts and given new life. They are a new creation and have become new. The drug addict is instantly and miraculously set free from his addiction because of this encounter and the college student is set free from his own pride and feels a supernatural calling into ministry.

There are countless testimonies such as these. I'm sure those of you who are reading this have either had a similar experience or know of others who have. These are testimonies of God's grace, love, and power that make us want to follow and praise Him forever. Someone who was once dead in sin has come to life; someone who was once blind can now see; someone who was once a captive enslaved to sin is now set free to live his or her life with a newfound hope of a brighter, better future and an eternity with Jesus.

However, they are still on the discipleship journey. While they have been given a second chance at a relationship with God and their hearts and minds have now been cleansed from all sin, they also have a life of choices to make ahead of them. They can still make choices that will affect their relationship with God and how they grow. They can still make choices that will have an eternal impact. This is why the discipleship process is so crucial in developing a life with God that is founded on loving Him with all of our being. Discipleship helps us along the journey toward our destiny. It helps us to learn how to love God and love people. Let's take a look at how new life plays a part in the discipleship process and how we should not take for granted the new life in Christ that we have.

Chapter 13

Practicing Discipleship

Jesus has called us to be His disciples for the rest of our lives. Accepting this invitation will launch us on a journey that will help us accomplish the purpose God has for us. It will help us to love Him with everything that we are. Something to keep in mind is this: we have an entire journey with Christ ahead of us. We have a multitude of trials and challenges we will face that will affect our growth along the journey. What choices will we make during those challenges and trials? Will we choose to keep journeying with Christ, following His design for our life, or take our own path that is easier? What choices will we make to help us achieve our destiny? What choices will we make that affect the lives of others?

Paul wrote over thirteen different letters to Christians all over the world encouraging and teaching them the ways of Jesus. However, a large portion of them were written to correct their choices and behavior. They had been given new life and freedom from their sin when they chose to follow Jesus, but needed direction to help them become the people Jesus wanted them to be.

Just like them we need spiritual direction if we are to achieve the purpose that God has for us. There are three avenues of spiritual direction that are part of the discipleship process. The first is Scripture.

Scripture

Scripture is how we learn who God is and about the life Christ wants us to live. However, Scripture can be difficult to understand because it is a collection of writings that, while consistent and point to Jesus, are still written by different people with different personalities, in different cultures, over a span of 4000 years. We need help to understand it. That is where the second and third avenues of spiritual direction come in.

The Holy Spirit

The second avenue that spiritual direction occurs is from the person of the Holy Spirit. The role of the Holy Spirit is to convict of sin (John 16:8), to reveal the truth and meaning of Scripture (John 14:26), and to empower us to be better witnesses. (Acts 1:8). Once we have responded to His conviction by repenting and becoming Jesus's disciples, He then helps us on the journey by teaching us what it means to be His disciple by helping us understand scripture, revealing who Jesus is, and transforming us into the people He designed us to be. This is the discipleship process called sanctification and is the way the Holy Spirit purifies our hearts along the journey. As we follow Him and listen to His voice, He reveals the areas of our lives that still need His help to be cleansed, and teaches us to submit to the process.

The Church

The third avenue of spiritual direction that God uses to teach us is the church. God has placed people with specific gifts of ministry in the church to fulfill their role to equip disciples of Jesus with what they need to grow. Paul emphasizes this in Ephesians 4:11-16 saying,

"He Himself gave some to be apostles, some prophets, some evangelists, and some pastors and teachers, for the equipping of the saints for the work of ministry, for the edifying of the body of Christ, till we all come to the unity of the faith and of the knowledge of the Son of God, to a perfect man, to the measure of the stature of the fullness of Christ; that we should no longer be children, tossed to and fro and carried about with every wind of doctrine, by the trickery of men, in the cunning craftiness of deceitful plotting, but, speaking the truth in love, may grow up in all things into Him who is the head, Christ, from whom the whole body, joined and knit together by what every joint supplies, according to the effective working by which every part does its share, causes growth of the body for the edifying of itself in love" (NKJV).

God uses all three of these avenues of spiritual direction together to help His people grow into mature disciples. Utilizing all three is crucial in the discipleship process because they help give new life and understanding. If one is left unused, then there is potential to be "tossed to and fro and carried along with every wind of doctrine" which basically means there won't be a solid foundation of truth built for us to build our lives on. Jesus emphasizes this when He challenges His disciples to build their lives upon His teachings. He says in Matthew 7:24-27,

"everyone then who hears these words of mine and does

them will be like a wise man who built his house on the rock. And the rain fell, and the floods came, and the winds blew and beat on that house, but it did not fall, because it had been founded on the rock. And everyone who hears these words of mine and does not do them will be like a foolish man who built his house on the sand. And the rain fell, and the floods came, and the winds blew and beat against that house, and it fell, and great was the fall of it" (NKJV).

When we become disciples of Jesus and are given new life, He wants our lives from that point on to be built upon His teachings and the truth.

Once we have been made a new creation, we are a clean slate. We have to immediately start this process of building a life that is firmly built upon Him. Jesus calls this process of building a foundation upon Him "abiding." He states in John 15:9-10, "as the Father loved Me, I also have loved you; abide in My love. If you keep My commandments, you will abide in My love, just as I have kept My Father's commandments and abide in His love" (NKJV). Jesus is our example of how to love the Father and obey His commands. If we abide in response to His love that we have experienced, we are given the new life that we need to continue to obey His commands.

INVITED TO ABIDE

The truth of the gospel is also this: not only do we gain salvation, freedom, and new life when we choose to accept the invitation to become His disciples, we also gain the grace and power we need to live exactly as God wants us to while we are still alive. Becoming a new creation is the first step along the journey with Him. We are given new life so that we can let go of the past and our bondage to sin to become His disciples and learn to love and obey Him. As we abide in Him, obeying His commands and remaining in His love as He teaches us in John 15, He reveals Himself to us. He helps us understand the truth of who He is and establishes a relationship with us as Lord and Friend.

As we develop this relationship with Him, our love for Him grows. As we spend time with Him, we take on His nature with the help and empowerment of the Holy Spirit. We will see the fruit of the Spirit grow in our lives. These fruits are characteristics of God Himself. He is the author and perfect representation of love, joy, peace, patience, kindness, goodness, faithfulness, gentleness, and self-control (Galatians 5:22-23). As we learn to be His followers and let Him do the work in us, we will manifest these traits as well. Where before our natural fleshly tendency might have been to live in hate, anger, selfish desires, lust, etc., we will now be able to resist those temptations, seeing the truth, and living like Christ. Where before some might have felt like giving up during the hard season, we can now clearly see the truth and it helps us endure the challenges. God wants to not only use those hard situations to grow and bless us, but also to build His kingdom and show His glory as He leads us through the trials. Because we understand this truth, we can endure those trials joyfully, just like Christ endured the cross joyfully for us, knowing that the trials and suffering would lead to the promised salvation and perfection and Kingdom expansion.

Unfortunately, there will be times when we make the wrong choices along our journey. It is important to remember this truth: repentance is still required even after salvation. We are all still fallen humans on a discipleship journey of learning how to love God with every part of our being. Because we are not yet completely perfected and still live in a fallen world, we still have potential to give in to temptation. However, when we abide in Jesus, remaining in His love and truth, we have a clear sight of how to resist temptation and are given the tools we need to resist the enemy who is trying to keep us from achieving our great destiny as Jesus's disciples. I mentioned three of those tools earlier: Scripture, the Holy Spirit, and the Church. Scripture teaches us how to resist the enemy with the truth. The Holy Spirit gives us power, discernment, and wisdom to know how to respond to temptation and cleanses and strengthens us, so we don't want to sin anymore. The church provides us with the encouragement and strength that we need to know we are not alone in the fight.

There are other principles that we need to remember that will also prepare us to endure the journey to become mature disciples who love God with all of our hearts, souls, and strength and who love others as much as ourselves. These principles help us to find new life when we are weak and help us to continue to abide in Christ every day. The first is this: God wants to give disciples of Jesus new life daily by renewing their minds every day.

Chapter 14

The Renewed Mind

As disciples of Jesus, we are on a journey to become more like Him so that we can become mature in Him. This journey, while filled with great transformation, peace, joy, and love, is also filled with many challenges and trials that will affect that walk unless we remain in His truth and love. These challenges will cause great stress and discouragement in our lives unless we train our minds and hearts to endure them. We know that God's plan is for us to thrive in every area of our lives but sometimes we need some spiritual direction to help us learn how to follow this plan.

How many of us struggle with anxiety, depression, loneliness, fear, doubt, confusion, etc. even as followers of Jesus? A lot of us don't know how to understand and control these negative emotions, letting them rule us. The answer is found in a life with Jesus. An invitation to discipleship is an invitation to new life or restoration not just when we first become His disciples but also throughout the journey we are on.

I also think of the word rejuvenate. God wants to

restore and rejuvenate those who follow Him. The enemy who comes to steal, kill, and destroy might try to bring us down by throwing things at us that wear us down and cause great emotional and physical distress. We might also be experiencing pain that comes from growth, which is still stressful. No matter what we are facing God wants to create new life inside of those who are His disciples so that we won't be worn down by these challenges.

A perfect illustration of this is an old couch that has tears and stains in it. It is worn down by constant use and abuse and needs to be restored. Someone with the skill can take it and make it new again. This is what God wants to do with us. We might have become worn down by the life that we live, but God wants to take what is torn and stained and repair it, making it better than it was before. He has the skill because He is the Master Restorer and Creator. Accepting the invitation to discipleship means that we also accept His invitation into new life. He wants to revive us when we are defeated, restore us when we are broken, and rejuvenate us when we are tired.

Paul emphasizes the need for rejuvenation in Romans 12:2 saying, "and do not be conformed to this world, but be transformed by the renewing of your mind, that you may prove what is that good and acceptable and perfect will of God" (NKJV). He also encourages us that God wants to renew us daily by saying in 2 Corinthians 4:16 "therefore we do not lose heart. Even though our outward man is perishing, yet the inward man is being renewed day by day" NKJV). Even though the world might respond to challenges in a way that causes them to lose heart, we have the opportunity to allow God to renew our minds and give us new life daily. However, accepting this invitation into daily renewal and new life only comes when we accept His invitation into

His presence and love. Experiencing His love is what brings transformation and is the ground where growth can occur. Experiencing His love when we seek His presence daily is what allows us to gain new life every day.

RENEWAL PRACTICES

There are a few spiritual practices that allow us to encounter His love and presence and experience daily renewal. I mentioned two of them in another chapter: praise and prayer. Both of these practices help us to encounter God's presence. When we develop the habit of practicing praise and prayer daily, these spiritual disciplines help us to experience daily rejuvenation when we encounter His presence and love in the deepest parts of our lives. Another principle that God wants to teach us that will allow us to experience new life is the spiritual practice of resting.

Invited to Rest

Jesus gives us a picture of what life as His disciples should look like in Matthew 11:28-30. He tells us, "Come to Me, all you who labor and are heavy laden, and I will give you rest. Take My yoke upon you and learn from Me, for I am gentle and lowly in heart, and you will find rest for your souls. For My yoke is easy and My burden is light" (NKJV). The word rest here is the Greek word *anapauō* which means "to cause or permit one to cease from any movement or labor in order to recover and collect his strength, to give rest, refresh, to give one's self rest, take rest, or to keep quiet, of calm and patient expectation."[1]

Being His disciples is not easy. There will be challenges along the journey to achieving our purpose. However, if we are yoked to Him, He will give us rest because His yoke is easy and the burden He gives us is light. He takes most of the load allowing us to lean back and rest.

I want to give an example of what this principle looks like. Airplane pilots are responsible for flying the aircraft long distances, usually filled with people. This might seem tiring because of the long flights. However, most larger aircraft have been equipped with autopilot allowing the pilots the chance to spend long trips resting while the plane does all of the work. It's the same in the discipleship process. We are responsible for the choices we make. However, when we give Jesus permission to rule our lives and bear the responsibility for helping us achieve our destiny, we can lean back and rest in Him, trusting Him to lead us, as well as handling all of the work that goes on in the discipleship and transformation process. Learning to rest allows us to experience rejuvenation throughout the journey. When we rest, we give God the freedom to create new life within us.

Resting For The Race

We are in a race. It's not a sprint though, it's a marathon. A marathon that we have to endure until we die, or Jesus comes back. Marathons require hard training and establishing healthy habits. When training to run a marathon, athletes have a rigorous exercise schedule. But they always pause from their busy routines to take a day to rest and give their muscles a chance to recuperate. As followers of Jesus, it is important that we do the same. This is why God gave the children of Israel the command to "remember the Sabbath day by keeping it holy" establishing the day of rest that we see in Exodus 20:8-11. Let's look at what God says:

> "Remember the Sabbath day, to keep it holy. Six days you shall labor and do all your work, but the seventh day is the Sabbath of the Lord your God. In it you shall do no work: you, nor your son, nor your daughter, nor your male servant, nor your female servant, nor your cattle, nor your stranger who is within your gates. For in six days the Lord made the heavens and the earth, the sea, and all that is in them, and rested the seventh day. Therefore, the Lord blessed the Sabbath day and hallowed it" (NKJV).

The practice of Sabbath that God instituted here was a way to help the people of Israel to learn how to rest. He rested on the seventh day of creation as a model for us to follow. Sabbath, or *šabāt* in Hebrew, is translated as to cease, desist, or put an end to.[2] In other words Sabbath simply means stop. It implies pausing from your daily routine in order to refocus on what is most important and rejuvenate yourself. God stopped on the seventh day and implemented Sabbath rest as a way to teach us to learn to pause in order to prevent the challenges we go through from causing unneeded problems in our lives. It is also a way to pause from the busy routines of life and refocus on what's most important, Him.

As I talked about in the first chapter His plan is that we thrive. Approaching these challenges and our daily routines without learning to rest causes issues and prevents us from truly thriving. Pausing when our lives get busy and we get overwhelmed gives us the chance to refocus and re-energize our spirits to be able to continue to follow Jesus well, loving Him with all of our being.

Let The Teacher Teach

In scripture, there is a story that teaches us the importance of pausing from our busy lives in order to focus on Jesus. In Luke 10:38-42, Jesus was visiting His friends Mary and Mary, the same sisters from the story in John 11 where Lazarus was raised from the dead. Martha was busy being a good hostess, cleaning and preparing the meal in order to serve Jesus. Mary, on the other hand, was sitting at Jesus' feet listening to Him as He talked with her, teaching the truth of Scripture. Martha got offended at Mary for not helping and asked Jesus to tell her to help her serve. Jesus's response is very important in understanding the need to stop what we are doing and focus on Him. He says to Martha in verse 41-42, "Martha, Martha, you are worried and troubled about many things. But one thing is needed, and Mary has chosen that good part, which will not be taken away from her" (NKJV).

Just like Martha was so focused on doing things to serve Jesus, we live our lives doing things in His name to serve Him. However, there is one thing many of us miss: serving Jesus is not the most important thing; resting in Him is. An invitation to rest in Him is an invitation to pause in our lives from the busyness, sit at His feet in a moment of stillness, and allow Him to teach us or just be with Him in the peace of His presence. An invitation to rest is an invitation to pause, take in the truth of what Jesus wants to teach and create in us, and allow ourselves to experience His love that brings transformation and purpose. This is how we thrive as His disciples, loving Him and others well.

Pause and Reflect

In the Psalms, there is a word that we can also learn a lesson from. That word is *selah* which also means "to pause." It's actually a musical term. There is a break in the music for reflection on what is being sung. The point of *selah* is to allow the truth of who God is that we are singing about to sink in so that we can respond to it with heartfelt praise and adoration. As I've mentioned before, praise is an important spiritual discipline to have as we learn how to become who God has called us to be. Taking the time to pause what we are doing to reflect on God, remembering who God is, and praising Him for what He has done and will do is extremely important in the discipleship process.

Abide

Pausing to reflect and remember also allows us to continue to abide. I talked about abiding earlier in this chapter. This principle of resting goes hand in hand with abiding. When we abide in Him our foundation remains secure. Pausing and reflecting allows our relationship with Him and love for Him to grow as we abide, allows our praise to be deeper, and allows us to be aware of His presence in our lives, growing us and shaping us to be like Him.

Pause to Repent

I was talking to a friend one day who asked this question: "how do I know if I'm in God's will, and if I'm not, how do I get back in His will?" As I talked with him, I discovered that he had made a decision to make a major change in his life for his own emotional health. However, he was questioning this decision and was having a hard time figuring out if it was actually God's will or not.

This is one question that I have heard over and over. I have asked this question myself several times. This time was different, though, because in that moment, the Holy Spirit spoke to me and said something that changed my view of past decisions. He said that sometimes when we are doubting decisions and feeling regret or shame, it is actually an invitation to stop what we are doing in order to repent and grow instead of dwelling on the negative emotion. It is an invitation to learn to pause from whatever we're doing to make ourselves feel better and examine the root of the problem. Why did we do what we did?

Pausing in the moment of insecurity, doubt, regret, or whatever negative emotion we are feeling allows us to take a step back and examine the decision to determine whether we were following God or not. If we were, then we move forward in peace, knowing we are on the right path. If not, we can realize our mistakes, repent, and get back on the right path, learning from them so we never do them again.

In the rest of this section, I am going to speak directly to those who are struggling with doubting or feeling shame for a decision. This section is more for those who are not in God's plan than those who already know they are in God's will. Even though we have been given new life when we become Jesus's disciples, we are still responsible for the choices we make moving forward on the journey. We can still make choices that are not part God's design, decisions that are not the best for our lives. You might be someone who left God's plan unintentionally or intentionally and are feeling regret and guilt. You might feel like you can't trust yourself anymore, causing you to feel depressed. That guilt and shame might cause you to keep from pursuing God's plan. However, God's intention is for us to let go of our own ways of doing things and follow Him. How can we get to the point where we can trust ourselves to make the decisions God wants us to?

The answer is simple, but comes at a cost of our own comfort. Seeing our own flaws and the need for change is hard. However, to truly be like Christ means accepting His invitation into transformation. God's invitation to us is an invitation to pause, examine our lives to see where we need Him, and repent for doing things our own way instead of His. This pause allows us to see what we need to do to make sure it never happens again. It also gives us the chance to experience His love that leads to repentance once again. This love will lead us to new life again as well. He gives us multiple chances to get back on track.

Chapter 15

How's Your Foundation

When I was talking to my friend that I mentioned in the last chapter, something else that the Holy Spirit spoke to me in this moment is that in the moments where we need to pause, He is also inviting us to examine our foundation. In Matthew 7:24-27 Jesus states,

> "Everyone then who hears these words of mine and does them will be like a wise man who built his house on the rock. And the rain fell, and the floods came, and the winds blew and beat on that house, but it did not fall, because it had been founded on the rock. And everyone who hears these words of mine and does not do them will be like a foolish man who built his house on the sand. And the rain fell, and the floods came, and the winds blew and beat against that house, and it fell, and great was the fall of it" (NKJV).

When we become a new creation, we have to build our lives upon Jesus. Sometimes we go through storms that have the potential to damage our foundations and cause us to question, be afraid, or begin to worry or doubt. When we go through storms or situations and experience those negative emotions, how do we react?

How many of us make worse decisions to try to "fix" the problem and make ourselves feel better? These decisions might make us happy for a moment, but if they aren't what God wants us to do, they will just make the situation worse. The reason for these reactions might be because our foundation that we built has been cracked and we no longer trust the truth. I experienced this myself a few years ago. I made decisions to try to replace the dream position I had lost, but they were the wrong decisions, made out of my own desires rather than what God intended. These decisions made me more and more frustrated and disillusioned until I finally stopped and let go of everything.

Something to consider when questioning our decisions is this: what caused the decision to become necessary. In my friend's case, he had made his decision for his own emotional health. While this decision wasn't necessarily a bad thing, the question he actually needed to ask himself was "why am I emotionally unhealthy?" If we figure out what is causing the emotional stress and fix the root cause, we might not need to try to do things to alleviate the discomfort.

I had to ask the same question myself when I went through my season of discontent. I made choices that weren't what God wanted me to do. I made these choices with good intentions, but I still had to examine myself to see why I was making them. It took me stopping and examining my own life and emotions in order to realize that I wasn't following Christ the way He had designed me to. I was making choices from my own needs and desire to make myself feel better rather than following Him. Once I realized that, I was able to make the necessary adjustments to restore my emotional and spiritual health and learn to follow Jesus the way He had designed me to.

A lot of us can blame our own health (or lack thereof) for the decisions we make, whether that be emotional, financial, spiritual, physical, or relational. But what causes healthiness (or lack of health) in the first place? Your foundation. If you want to be physically healthy, your foundation will be built on a life of exercise and healthy eating. For emotional health, it's about doing what makes you happy. The list goes on. However, a life built on things that aren't Jesus is always destined to fall apart at some point. Only a life built on Jesus is stable. Building on any other "truths" or quick fixes is like building a house on sand. Most people miss the fact that if you're unhealthy in one area, it will impact all of the other areas of life. If you're spiritually unhealthy, then eventually the foundation you've built your emotional health on will shatter. If you're emotionally unhealthy then your spiritual life isn't firm either, and you will be led by your emotions instead of truth. That's why it's so important to build your entire life on Christ, not just one or two areas. That way, when you start to question your decisions and why you do the things you do, you can rest knowing that your foundation is firm. Knowing you are following God the way He designed you to, you can remain at peace and thrive in every area of life. However, if our lives aren't built upon Jesus, when the storms, doubts, temptations, etc. come, we will react the wrong way and quickly fall apart.

Take the Time To Examine Your Foundation

So how do we get to the place where our entire life is built on Christ so that when the storms come the foundation doesn't crack? The answer to this is found in God's invitation to rest. We must take the time in our lives to pause and look at our foundation. Before you buy a house, an inspector comes and inspects the building itself and the foundation it's built on. If the foundation is cracked and can't be fixed, it's not worth buying. Fortunately, our foundations can be fixed no matter how badly damaged. However, just like a new prospective homeowner must be willing to first have the house inspected and then be willing to fix the problems if they want to buy it, we must choose to first allow ourselves to pause in order to examine ourselves and then implement certain things in our lives to fix it. We can't just keep going, expecting things in our lives to work out, without making sure the foundation our lives are built on is secure.

Saul, or Paul as we know him, is the perfect example of someone who had a bad foundation that he thought was good until he came to the point where he was forced to pause and examine his life. Saul was a dedicated Pharisee who spent his entire life studying the *torah* or the law. The law was the foundation his entire life was built on. The principles of the law were so ingrained into the Pharisees that they couldn't recognize Jesus for who He was, the Messiah. They were blinded by their religious dedication to their interpretation of the law rather than actually following God. Saul was so dedicated to his interpretation of the law that he persecuted and murdered those who followed Jesus, breaking the very law that he was so dedicated to: "you shall not murder" (Exodus 20:13). It took Jesus showing Himself to Paul, forcing him to stop and reflect on the truth to get him to realize the reality of his own deception. When he was persecuting Christians, he met Jesus in a dramatic encounter. That encounter changed his entire perspective and forced him to pause his life and beliefs in order to see the cracks in his foundation and allow God to fix them. When his foundation was fixed, he was given new life and went on to be the one who brought the gospel to the Gentiles. It's important to remember that it took him pausing his life in order to fix his foundation and then continuing on the correct path.

HOWS YOUR FOUNDATION

Let me ask you this question: "How's your foundation?" Stop and consider this question for a few minutes. Are there any cracks in the foundation of your life that you need Jesus to fix? What are they? My challenge is for all of us to constantly ask this question so that we can remain firm in Jesus. Make it a habit to pause and look at your foundation. In the example I used of my friend, in order to continue to follow Jesus, he had to pause and examine his foundation to determine the reason his emotional health was bad in the first place. I had to stop and examine my foundation to realize that it was cracked.

When we allow Jesus to fix the cracks in our foundation, giving our foundation new life, our entire lives change. As I told my friend, when our lives are built on Jesus, when we're sad we still have His joy to stand on. When we're lonely, we have a community, and the family of God to turn to. Also, when we're stressed, we have His peace. When we doubt, are insecure, and afraid we can allow His love to cast out our fear. Nothing can shake our lives when our foundation is whole and built upon Jesus. All it takes to remain whole is to accept His invitation to pause in the midst of the situation we're going through, examine our foundation, repent, and allow Him to fix the cracks, bringing new life into our lives. Then when we are faced with those negative emotions again that threaten who we are, our foundation is secure. We can then stand up knowing we are in His will with whatever decision we make.

Chapter 16

Enjoy Life With Jesus And Others

I have spent the last few chapters discussing how experiencing new life throughout the discipleship process helps us become more like Him. It's also extremely important to remember that new life is an absolute necessity in accomplishing God's plan for our lives. It is a major part of the discipleship process. We need to constantly renew ourselves in His presence if we are to succeed in anything on our journey with Him.

I want to end this section with one final thought. Experiencing new life and rejuvenation by developing systems where we integrate these spiritual practices into our daily lives gives us the chance to enjoy our life with Jesus. This is a deep, spiritual principle. New life where we have learned to rest and daily experience His love equals a happier, more joy and peace filled life, free from the worry and fear that we might experience during the challenges we face. When we've learned to consistently practice the spiritual disciplines that help us grow as well as taking time to pause and rest, we will be able to enjoy life with Christ more.

The same is true in our natural lives when we get

enough sleep, exercise, food, etc. All of these things help us to stay healthy in every area of life. Being healthy physically and emotionally allows us the ability to enjoy life. However, it is important to remember that while it is necessary for us to be physically and emotionally healthy and mature, it is much more necessary to be spiritually healthy and mature. Only by being spiritually healthy and mature can we learn to enjoy life in the other areas the way God wants and designed us to. Like I mentioned in a previous chapter, He has designed us to thrive in every area of life. All it takes is following His plan as we respond to His love by becoming His disciples.

Maturity in every area of life doesn't happen overnight, unfortunately, especially spiritual maturity. We must keep practicing these principles daily in order to keep experiencing God's love and presence which brings new life and transformation. We must continue to pause in our lives, even if we're serving Him, in order to refocus our attention on Him. We must continue to repent for the unbiblical mindsets we've allowed, and continue encountering His love so that we can experience new life. We must pause to let Him teach and transform us so that we can love Him the way He wants us to. Because new life and lasting rejuvenation only comes from following Jesus, those of us who have learned to pause to repent, pause to reflect, pause to praise Him, pause to invite Him into our lives, and pause to rest in Him are able to enjoy life with Jesus. When we are able to enjoy life with Jesus because we have been given new life daily, we come closer to maturity, able to love Him and others with every part of our lives, accomplishing the plan and purpose He designed us for. New life also allows us to take on the new identity that He has for us. We will talk about this over the next few chapters.

Part 3 A New Identity

Therefore, if anyone is in Christ, he is a new creation; old things have passed away; behold, all things have become new.

2 Corinthians 5:17

Chapter 17

Invited Into Identity

Jesus is inviting us to experience His love and discover our God given purpose to love Him with all of our hearts and to love others as ourselves. When we respond to that love by becoming His disciples, giving Him our lives, we step into a journey of new life. This journey sets us on a path of transformation through discipleship. It is a journey of experiencing His love daily in a way that rejuvenates us and allows us to grow. Something that is important to remember on this journey, though, is that an invitation to follow Jesus is also an invitation into a new identity.

WHAT IS YOUR NAME?

We all have a name that we have had since birth. This name is associated with your identity. My name, for instance, is Benton James Ward. But that isn't my full identity. My identity is this: My name is Benton James Ward. I am a son. I am a brother and an uncle. I am a new husband. I smile a lot, cannot frown, and I laugh very loudly at everything. I am a writer who has published a book and is working on more. I am a musician who likes to write songs. I am also very friendly, a "flaming extrovert" as some of my friends have lovingly called me. I am very passionate about truth and integrity. I also have some not so great traits. I am very critical of people and their unwise decisions sometimes (not my best character trait admittedly). I get frustrated a lot at people who do things I don't agree with. I sometimes am very opinionated, especially when I am frustrated at people's less than wise decisions. Above all of the character traits that make up my identity, the most important thing about me is this: I am a follower of Jesus.

All of these characteristics describe me. They make up who I am. When people hear the name Benton, BJ, or Beej, as my friends and family call me, they immediately think of all these characterizations that define who I am, especially my loud laugh, and that I am a follower of Jesus. This is my identity.

What is your name? Who are you? Some of you might have some of the same characterizations. You might be a son or daughter, wife or husband, aunt, or uncle. You might be funny, like to smile and laugh, or have no humor at all. Whoever you are, people will think of the defining attributes of your identity and character when they hear your name.

In looking at our identity, there is something that we need to remember. We have a different identity before we become disciples of Jesus. Even though we are created in the image of God, we are self-focused, prideful, unable to be the people God originally designed us to be because we are corrupted by sin. This identity leads to a destiny of death.

We are doomed to eternal punishment, separated from God forever. Because we live in a fallen world, some have the identity of orphan, beggar, thief, murderer, cheater, liar, poor, broken, disabled, grumpy, mean, etc. Unfortunately, because we still have a sinful nature, we can also maintain those negative aspects from our former identity even as followers of Jesus unless we allow Him to cleanse our identity and mature us. I'll talk about this more later in this chapter.

What weaknesses do you have, mistakes that you've made in the past caused by your sinful nature that have led to a negative identity? As I said before, I am very critical of people who I disagree with who just don't seem to want to listen to what I have to say. I also like to be right and I will argue my point until the other person agrees with me or I finally concede that I'm wrong. This trait comes from my sinful nature of pride. Even though I have followed Jesus as long as I can remember, I still have things that I struggle with. They are part of who I am.

Unfortunately, we all have sinful characteristics that are part of who we are as fallen creations. Some of us might be liars, adulterers, cheaters, or thieves. Some of us might have addictions that we can't defeat. Some of us might be afraid of everything, filled with anxiety, sadness, or depression. Some of us might be filled with pride, lust, or anger that causes us to do things we're not proud of.

The reality is these weaknesses are a part of our identity because of our sin nature. Sin keeps us from achieving the purpose God has for us and becoming the person God created us to be. However, there's something important to remember, though, that will give us hope. These sinful characteristics were never God's plan for us. Even though we have them, they are not supposed to be part of our life story and the destiny God designed us to have. In order for us to have the destiny God wants us to have, we need a new name. One that He gives us. An identity made up of traits that He creates within us as we follow Him, no matter what our past sinful identities are.

A NEW NAME

Accepting Jesus's invitation to discipleship means that we are "baptized in the name of the Father, Son, and the Holy Spirit" Matthew 28:19. The word "baptized" here is the Greek word *baptizo* which means "to submerge completely" and "to cleanse by washing."[1] The word "name" is the word *onoma* which means "the identity used for everything the name covers, everything the thought or feeling of which is around in the mind by mentioning, hearing, and remembering."[2]

What this means is that, as His disciples, Jesus wants us to be submerged in and cleansed by His identity until there is nothing left of our old selves. In this moment of purification we take on His identity as well. Water baptism is one of the ordinances of the church that we as Christians practice to symbolize the process of what happens when we are baptized into the identity of Christ. Water baptism demonstrates outwardly what's happening inside of us. When we are submerged in Him, we die to ourselves, are buried in a watery grave, are resurrected in Him, and given new life. As a new creation we are given a new identity because our former identity of sin is now buried and dead. We have a new life ahead of us. God has an identity and a new name He wants us to be known as, but we have the choice to take on that identity or to live as we want to.

So, what identity does God have in mind for us? To

know this, it is important to look at Scripture. What does God say about the identity He has planned for us? I'd like to talk about a few that are important to remember over the next few chapters.

Chapter 18

New Names

We all have an identity, a name that people know us as. There are characteristics that we have that people associate with our name. For instance, I am a husband, uncle, son, and brother. I am also an extroverted musician and writer who loves to laugh, smile, and joke around. Most importantly, I am a follower of Jesus. This is my identity. You might have similar characteristics that are associated with your identity.

Unfortunately, because of our sin nature, we also have negative characteristics that are associated with who we are. Like me, you might be arrogant, opinionated, and have to be right all of the time. Maybe you're struggling with an addiction, sexual sin, or depression. You might be angry and bitter at everyone in your life. Whatever weakness and sinful characteristics you have know this: your sin struggles were never part of God's plan or design for you. Fortunately, there is a way for you to become new. All it takes is for you to experience His love for you and accept His invitation to become His disciple. Once you accept this invitation and step into the journey of discipleship, your former identity, what you were known for before Christ, is dead and gone, unless you pick it up again. You have a choice ahead of you. Will you allow the old ways and identities to stay dead or will you choose to resurrect them and remain as you once were?

If you choose to follow Jesus as His disciple you are given a new identity. Discovering this identity will help you accomplish the purpose that God has designed you for. It will help you love Him with all of your being and love people as yourself. Let's talk about a few of the names that God has for us when we become His disciples.

New Creation

One of the most important identities that God gives us when we become His followers is that we are a "new creation." I talked about this in the last section, but I want to emphasize something in this chapter to stress the importance of this principle. Paul tells the Corinthians and us in 2 Corinthians 5:17, "therefore, if anyone is in Christ, he is a new creation; old things have passed away; behold, all things have become new." Paul is saying that if we are in Christ, baptized in His identity, abiding in His teaching and presence, cleansed by His Spirit, we are given the name and identity of "New Creation." Our former identity is no longer how God sees us. The attributes we were formerly known for when people hear our names are now dead and gone. When we accept this identity and live our lives as a new creation every day, through renewing our minds daily in His presence and through reading scripture, God can now begin to create the other character traits that make up our identity. He wants us to be known as people who walk in the fruit of the spirit: "love, joy, peace, long-suffering, kindness, goodness, faithfulness, gentleness, self-control" (Galatians 5:22-23, NKJV) rather than the fruit of the flesh: "adultery, fornication, uncleanness, lewdness, idolatry, sorcery, hatred, contentions, jealousies, outbursts of wrath, selfish ambitions, dissensions, heresies, envy, murders, drunkenness, revelries, and the like" (Galatians 5:19-21, NKJV). These were the characteristics of our old identity when we were bound to sin. The fruit of the Spirit are the characteristics of our new identity in Him. These traits are what He wants us to be known for when people hear our names. He wants us to be known as people who love Him with all of our being and who love each other as much as we love ourselves. This is our identity in Him. It all starts with taking on the identity of New Creation every day, letting Him renew our minds as we follow Him, allowing ourselves to be baptized in His identity.

Disciple of Jesus

In the beginning of this book I talked about how, when we accept God's invitation to respond to His love, we become His disciple. I want to talk about this a bit further in this chapter, emphasizing that when we become Jesus's disciple, we don't just call ourselves His disciple. Calling ourselves a Christian isn't enough. We must take on the identity of His disciple. The word disciple means "student" or "apprentice."

What do you think of when you hear the word "student?" I think of the process that I just completed to get my masters in pastoral counseling. I was a graduate student for a year, going through the learning process to further my education and start a new career. I dedicated myself to reading, writing papers, studying, and taking tests in order to learn and advance my career. You also might think of children who are still in school. These elementary, middle, and high school students are learning what they need to prepare them for adulthood. In order to be mature adults in today's society they need to go to school and learn from trained teachers.

For disciples of Jesus, we become His students for life. This means we surrender to Him, laying down our goals and dreams in order to learn from the Master Teacher. Just like my identity for a year was that of a graduate student, we who love Jesus and follow Him take on the lifelong identity of "student." Because we are finite and have limited knowledge, we should be constantly learning from the One who has all knowledge and wisdom. There are a few qualities that we must have as His students to truly take on the identity of a disciple. I want to talk about three very important ones:

1. We must be teachable.

Humility is one of the most important traits of those who take on the identity of "student of Jesus." Humility allows us to recognize that we don't know everything, but He does. It also allows us to see our limitations and see that we need His help to grow. It allows us to submit to the discipleship process, learning what it means to be a follower of Jesus and who He desires us to be. Those who are not teachable will never grow and will never achieve the purpose He has for them.

2. We must be willing to suffer and go through hard trials gladly.

God never promised us that life as His students will be easy. In fact, Jesus says the opposite. He tells those who follow Him that we will be hated, mocked, persecuted, and even put to death for following Him (Matthew 10:22). There will be many trials that we must endure along the journey. However, James and Paul both tell us to be glad when going through these trials, knowing that they will lead to growth and perfection (Romans 5:3-5, James 1:2-4). It might be difficult, and even unreasonable to some, but part of how we learn and grow as His students is through pain and suffering. These trials will look differently for everyone. Some might have to endure physical pain and even death, while others might endure emotional pain that comes from experiencing loss, growing pains, or other kinds of emotional pain. However, we must always remember two things. First, no matter what form the suffering takes, it will always lead to growth, blessings, and eternal reward. Second, He is always with us through the process, helping and strengthening us.

This is why we must always be glad to endure those trials and suffering. God has our perfect future in mind when He leads us through suffering, teaching us to endure. In fact He Himself is our model that we can follow for how to go through trials and suffering willingly. I talked about this in an earlier chapter. Jesus Himself endured trials and suffering that most of us will never have to go through. He did it gladly and joyfully knowing that the end result of His suffering would be our salvation and the growth of His eternal Kingdom. He is a God who is willing to suffer with His people. He suffered so that we would know that we can do it because He did it and is with us, helping us.

3. We must love.

Love is the distinguishing trait of a disciple of Jesus. Jesus says that people would know that we follow Him if we love Him, following His teaching obediently, and love others (John 14:15, John 13:35). This principle is what this book is about. As I stated in a previous chapter, love motivates us to become who He wants us to be and achieve our destiny. If we want to take on the name of "disciple of Jesus" and be known as His students, we must love.

Child of God

Another identity that God gives us is "Child of God". Paul tells us in Ephesians 1 that God's plan has always been to adopt us as His children when we follow Jesus and allow ourselves to be baptized in His identity. He says in verses 5 and 6 of Ephesians 1 that God "predestined us to adoption as sons by Jesus Christ to Himself, according to the good pleasure of His will, to the praise of the glory of His grace, by which He made us accepted in the Beloved." Paul also states in Romans 8:16 that "the Spirit Himself bears witness with our spirit that we are children of God" (NKJV). When we follow Jesus and abide in Him, the Holy Spirit bears witness that our adoption into the family of God is complete. In this moment we become His sons and daughters. As His sons and daughters, we are given access to Him not only as our Lord but as our Father, deepening our relationship with Him. I talked about this in an earlier chapter. When we accept this identity that He has for us we not only know Him as Lord, but as Father. When we know Him as Father, taking on the identity that He has for us as son and daughter, we can love and obey Him more completely.

Heirs of God

As sons and daughters of God, He also calls us His heirs. After emphasizing that we are God's children in Romans 8:16, Paul continues in the next verse saying, "and if children, then heirs, heirs of God and joint heirs with Christ, if indeed we suffer with Him, that we may also be glorified together" (NKJV). God is King of Kings and Lord of Lords. As His sons and daughters, we are given an inheritance and title as a joint ruler with Jesus. Notice, though, that we have to be willing to suffer with Him here on the earth, one of the traits of being His disciple that I mentioned earlier. We are glorified with Him, given positions and identities as joint rulers with Christ, after enduring the suffering and trials we must go through as His disciples.

Because we have been given titles and an inheritance, we also have to realize that this also means that we have the power and authority that goes along with being His heir. Before the fall in Genesis, humanity was given authority to rule the earth for God. But, unfortunately, Adam and Eve gave it up to Satan when they disobeyed God. God's plan is to redeem us, restoring us to our rightful positions in His kingdom. We have been given power and authority to take dominion once again through Jesus. Paul tells us in Romans 8:11 that the same power that raised Jesus from the dead lives inside of us. We have been given authority to walk in the same power that Jesus did on the earth. Jesus tells us that in His name, we have the power to cast out demons, speak with new tongues, take up serpents and drink poison and not be harmed, heal the sick, and raise the dead (Mark 16: 17-18, Luke 10:19-20). All authority has been given to Him and He grants this authority to us to use. I will talk about this empowerment in the next chapter, but I want to emphasize that authority and power are part of our identity as God's children. We have been given authority over the forces of darkness that dominate this world, seeking to kill, steal, and destroy. We are called to conquer these forces as well as the sin within us with His help as we follow Him. This is our identity when we take on the name "Heir of God."

More Than Conquerors

As God's children, through Jesus we have been given authority and power to fight against the forces of darkness that threaten to keep us bound to sin. We have been given power through Jesus and the Holy Spirit within us to fight our sin nature as well, resisting temptation and overcoming what enslaves us. Paul tells us in Romans 8:37 that through Jesus "we are more than conquerors." This means that we have been given the identity of "More than Conqueror." Think about that. Think of what the word conqueror means. The Greek word that Paul uses here is the word *hypernikaō* which means "to vanquish beyond" or "to gain a decisive victory."[1] Each of us who have been baptized into Jesus's identity and now identify as His disciples are meant to take on the identity and name of "More than Conqueror," someone who is able to completely and utterly vanquish any enemy, whether demonic or sin nature, through the power of the Holy Spirit and the Name of Jesus that we have access to. Picture what this looks like. What comes to mind is a scene in the final Lord of the Rings movie, *Return of the King*, when Aragorn, the rightful king of Gondor, enters the fight for Gondor with the army of the dead. They wipe out every enemy in their path without breaking a sweat. Complete and utter victory. God has the power to conquer any enemy without breaking a sweat. In fact, He's already won because of Jesus's victory on the cross. We already have been given overwhelming, ultimate victory through Jesus.

However, sometimes our eyes have to be opened to the truth of how God has already won. Some people don't understand this and walk around defeated by their situations. This is not the identity that God wants us to be known as. We need to accept the fact that we have already won. He gives us complete victory over sin and the enemy, naming us "More than Conquerors." We must accept the names that He gives us through Christ Jesus and live our lives victorious, taking authority over the things that once held us captive. Only by accepting the names and identities that He gives as the reality of who we are can we achieve the purpose that He has for us.

Chapter 19

Accept Your Identity

God has a new name for us when we accept His invitation to follow Him. We have been named "New Creation," "Disciple of Jesus," "Child of God," "Heir of God,"and "More than conqueror." However, there is an enemy who wants to keep us from accepting our identity in Christ, blinding us with lies. If we do not understand these identities that we have in Christ, we will be easy prey for this enemy and will remain bound, never able to truly fulfill the destiny that God has for us. Because we are still human and imperfect, still learning how to be like Christ in every area of our lives, we have to remain vigilant to what the enemy is trying to do in our minds. Our hearts might be in the right place, but our minds can still be easily swayed until we grow in maturity, able to recognize the methods that the enemy uses to keep us from seeing the truth. Our eyes need to be open to these methods used to deceive us into believing a lie, keeping us from taking on our identity in Christ.

How many of us have been following Jesus for years, but still struggle with addictions, shame, anxiety, fear, doubt, unbelief, depression, anger, etc.? How many of us stay bound to these former identities no matter how many years we've spent following Jesus? What's worse is that many of us have let those things control our lives to the point where we can no longer function healthily. How many of us have allowed these attributes to become our identity versus the identity that Jesus wants us to have?

You might be in a place in life where you don't believe that you're good enough to accomplish the purpose that God has for you, that you're too young or too old to do what God has called you to do. You might believe that your past or current struggles and sinful identity disqualify you from having a destiny or that you're not smart enough to do what God has put on your heart to do. You might believe that your looks aren't good enough, that you can't speak well enough, aren't rich enough, or are too poor to accomplish the purpose God has created you for. If you fit into one of these categories, it is important that you realize that this is not the identity that God has for you. God says these things about you:

You are fearfully and wonderfully made (Psalm 139).

God spent a lot of time thinking about how He wanted to create you and the identity He has for you. You don't need to be afraid that you aren't good enough or beautiful enough to have a destiny. He thinks you are because He created you to be. David gives us several practical lessons in Psalm 139 that we can apply to our lives as we journey to be like Christ. Verses 13-15 tell us that we are "fearfully and wonderfully made" by God. He formed our bodies, paying extra attention to each detail of our features so that we would be a "marvelous work." The word "fearfully" in this passage is the word *yārē* and means "to revere, to stand in awe of, and to cause astonishment or godly fear."[1] The words "wonderfully" and "marvelous" are both the word *pālâ* which means "to be distinct, to mark as different, be distinguished, and to be wonderful."[2] These words imply uniqueness.

What God is saying to us in this passage is that before we were born, He had a design in mind for each part of our bodies and crafted us with such intimate attention that it would cause all of creation to stand in awe and astonishment at what He created. How many of us have ever doubted that we are created exactly as God intended? How many of us have rejected what God says about our bodies and done things to change it in order to make ourselves happier? How many of us have lost hope because we never seemed to fit into our own body?

I feel like it is necessary to stop and explain myself further in order to avoid confusion and misinterpretation. I am not writing this to say that changing your body is always wrong. In our culture, tattoos, piercings, changing hairstyles, exercising to lose fat, are normal ways to change your body. There is nothing wrong with these. Exercising and dieting are healthy practices and can help you avoid health issues and maybe live longer. However, we have to examine the motives behind why we do them. If your motive is to express yourself and enjoy life, then by all means, do it. Your choice to cut your hair, pierce your tongue, or get a tattoo is between you and God. If it's not against scripture and you don't feel convicted by getting your haircut, then do it. Tattoos might be a little bit more of a controversial topic for some Christians, but in my opinion, which some might disagree with, that is a choice to make that is between you and God as well. If you want to build your muscles up to look like someone from the cover of People magazine, then do it. More power to you.

However, if the motive behind whatever you do to change your body is out of shame or insecurity, or to rebel against your parents or others, then I would challenge you to look at the root of why you feel the way you do. It's not your body that is the problem, it is the lie that you believe. This lie has become your identity. You don't need to change things about yourself to try to become something that you weren't created to be. He has a destiny for you, an identity that allows you to find your worth and value in Him.

> ***You have the Mind of Christ and the Holy Spirit giving you wisdom when you ask for it. (1 Corinthians 2:16, James 1:5)***

How many of us feel like we aren't smart enough or don't have the ability to fulfill the purpose God has for us? How many of us have become bound by this identity, held back by fear of failure? This is a lie as well. A lie that holds us back from the identity that God has for us as disciples who are more than conquerors. The Bible is very clear that wisdom comes from God and He gives it to us when we ask. Part of our identity is that we have the mind of Christ when we follow Him. We also have the Spirit of God who teaches us and helps us to understand as we learn. Moses thought that he couldn't speak well enough to be the one that God used to lead the children of Israel out of Egypt. But we see in Scripture that his perceived weakness never stopped him from taking on the identity that God had for him, standing up to Pharaoh and leading the Israelites on their way to the Promised Land. If fear is your identity, then allow the Holy

Spirit to open up your eyes to the truth that you are smart and capable enough in Christ. Paul tells us that we can do all things through Christ who gives us strength (Philippians 4:13).

You are invited to a higher and greater purpose than you realize (Jeremiah 1:5)

In Jeremiah 1:5, God speaks a message to Jeremiah that applies to all of us. He states, "Before I formed you in the womb, I knew you; Before you were born, I sanctified you; I ordained you a prophet to the nations." There are three things we can learn from this verse:

1. God formed us in the womb,
2. God knows who we are
3. God has a plan to use us to fulfill some great purpose.

However, to really grasp the importance of this story in defining our identities we have to look at the next few verses. Jeremiah responds to God by saying "Ah, Lord God! Behold, I cannot speak, for I am a youth" (Jeremiah 1:6).

Jeremiah, at this point hadn't realized or accepted the identity that God had for him. His identity was based on his inability to speak and his youth. How many of us have similar experiences? How many of us have said I'm not good enough, I'm too young, or I'm too old to be used by God? A lot of us have. But, we see that this is not the identity God has for us. God's response to Jeremiah shows us He doesn't see things the same way we do. He says to Jeremiah and to us, "Do not say, 'I am a youth, for you shall go to all to whom I send you, and whatever I command you, you shall speak.

Do not be afraid of their faces, for I am with you to deliver you,' says the Lord" (Jeremiah 1:8). After saying this He did something very important. He touched Jeremiah's mouth saying, "behold, I have put My words in your mouth. See, I have this day set you over the nations and over the kingdoms, to root out and to pull down, to destroy and to throw down, to build and to plant" (Jeremiah 1:10). A few verses later, He said to Jeremiah, "I am ready to perform my word" (Jeremiah 1:12).

Just like Jeremiah had to have God get in His face and do something dramatic to wake him up to the truth, some of us need this same wake up call. God wants to "touch our lips" with His love, inviting us through this experience to follow Him so that He can show us exactly who He has called us to be. Let's look again at what God says to Jeremiah after He touches His mouth. "Behold, I have put My words in your mouth. See, I have this day set you over the nations and over the kingdoms, to root out and to pull down, to destroy and to throw down, to build and to plant" (Jeremiah 1:10).

While not all of us are called to be prophets that God sets "over the nations and over the kingdoms, to root out and to pull down, to destroy and to throw down, to build and to plant" we still have a purpose in God's kingdom, a destiny He has given us to accomplish. Jeremiah's task was to be a prophet and to speak the words that God had given him to the nation. This is why the act of God touching His mouth was so important. He was showing Jeremiah that He was putting the words in His mouth. He was using the very thing that Jeremiah thought was the weakest part of Him. This shows us that He wants to redeem and empower what we perceive as weak, demonstrating His strength in our weakness. He emphasizes this to Paul in 2 Corinthians 12:9

saying, "My grace is sufficient for you, for My strength is made perfect in weakness" (NKJV).

Something else we can see from this is that God wasn't only redeeming Jeremiah's weakest part. He was also empowering the part of Him that He wanted to use. His mouth. Because He was giving Jeremiah the identity of a prophet, He was cleansing and anointing Jeremiah's mouth, the part of him that was the most useful tool that would allow him to achieve his purpose and take on this identity. What identity does God want you to have? What part of your life does God want to empower you to use?

His Workmanship

There is one more identity that God gives us as His disciples. Paul points it out in Ephesians 2:10 saying, "we are His workmanship, created in Christ Jesus for good works, which God prepared beforehand that we should walk in them" (NKJV). We have been created to do good works which God designed us for. Every part of us is created to do good works. However, those works might be different for each of us. God created each of us uniquely with specific traits and talents and wants to use what He created to achieve His purpose.

The story of Jeremiah emphasizes this principle. Jeremiah had a mouth and a tongue that God created, giving him the natural ability to speak. He just wasn't confident in this ability. He had to be empowered to use this ability and allow his way of thinking to be transformed so that he could be used. He had to allow God to transform His identity into that of a prophet. The same can be said of us. God has created us with hands, feet, a mouth, eyes, etc. that can be used. We just have to think differently about ourselves in order to see that we can be used. Our identity is that we are "God's Workmanship." We have been created to do good works with what God has given us.

What things are in your life already that God can use? What dreams, passions, and talents do you have that God created you with? God wants to use what He created within you to grow His kingdom. I'll talk more about this in the next section, but I want to emphasize this principle by saying that this is the identity that God has for us. If we don't understand that we are created to do the good works that He has prepared for us to do, we will never achieve the destiny He has for us. What would have happened if Jeremiah decided to keep his old identity? He would have stayed bound to fear and anxiety, believing that he wasn't good enough to achieve the destiny God had for him. How many of us today are bound to our old identities? How many of us are ok with staying bound because we don't understand that there is more available?

To accept our identity and the names that He calls us we must learn to stay submerged in Him. If we stay in His presence, practicing the spiritual disciplines that allow us to grow as His disciples, we can learn how to accept the identity that He has for us and allow Him to make us who He wants us to be through the power of His Holy Spirit.

Chapter 20

Submerged Identity

L ike I've said throughout this book, God has a plan for our lives that is greater than we can possibly imagine. He wants us to experience His love and respond to it by becoming His disciples, loving Him as Lord, Father, and Friend with all of our being, and taking on the identity that He has for us. All it takes is saying yes to His invitation, choosing to walk with Him as His disciples and letting Him make us who He wants us to be.

There is one more thing I want to talk about that is crucial for us to remain in the identity God has for us. Our entire identity is meant to be submerged in Christ's identity. This is how we fulfill our main purpose of loving Him with all of our hearts as His disciples. However, we have each been given a secondary purpose that helps us to achieve our primary purpose. This secondary purpose is part of our identity. For instance, I am a pastor. This calling is part of my identity. This is how I achieve my primary purpose of loving God and loving others. However, it is important that we remember that our secondary purpose is never to supersede our primary purpose. Another way to say this is this:

This secondary identity is never to supersede our primary identity of Disciple of Christ.

Let me give a personal example to illustrate my point. I mentioned earlier that I went through a season of discontent that almost brought me to the point of burnout. I had been forced to give up a dream that I had had for years and was searching to find my purpose and fill the hole in my life. At the time I was invited to be a young adults pastor at a church in Louisville, Ky. I knew that I was called to be a pastor and help people know Christ, so I took it. However, I also knew that this was temporary and that I would have to eventually figure out what to do with my life. While I knew that I was called to be a pastor, I wanted to know where I was meant to be in the future, who I was meant to be pastoring, and when I would be able to go back into full time ministry. I wasn't content where I was. Pastoring was my whole identity, and I wasn't content until I could pastor full time. I made plans to try to get back into full time ministry, thinking that that would fill the void that was left by the dream I had to give up. However, the plans that I made were never what God actually intended me to do and I never felt peace about them. Finally, after years of searching and planning, I hit the breaking point. I stopped and examined my life to figure out what I was doing wrong. It was at this moment that God spoke this to me "if you will let go of your identity as a pastor and follow me, I will lead you where I want you." It was at this moment that I discovered that my identity as a pastor had superseded the main identity that He had for me as "disciple of Jesus." I had forgotten how to simply follow Jesus and walk with Him. At that moment I realized that I had to let go of my dreams and learn to follow Christ. I resigned from my role as young adults pastor, said no to all of the plans I had made, and began a journey of simply learning how to be Jesus's disciple. Ever since then, God has opened my eyes to the identity that He has for me and given me new dreams and plans that will allow me to thrive as His disciple.

How many of us have done the same thing? You might be so caught up in doing the job that God has given you that you have forgotten your identity as a disciple of Jesus. You might even have accepted a position that God never meant for you in the first place because you put that identity above your identity as "disciple." Friends, here's something to think about. God wants us to first and foremost be His disciples, disciples whose lives are completely and permanently submerged in Him. When we are submerged in Him, our primary identity can only be His disciple. All other identities, whether it be pastor, doctor, lawyer, etc., are to be submerged as well, taking the place behind our identities as disciples of Jesus. When those identities supersede our identity as His disciples, we take our lives out of His plan and put them back on our own path. Walking down our own path leads to our destruction.

This almost happened to me and has happened to thousands of people in today's society. Thousands of pastors are leaving ministry because their main identity was pastor instead of disciple and they never learned to follow Him as He designed us to. Thousands of people are experiencing depression, loneliness, frustration etc. because they have chosen to identify more with their secondary purposes rather than their primary purpose. They never learned how to truly love God and love people, letting that love motivate them to follow Him as His disciples. They chose their own identities and positions rather than God's. This was never God's intention for us. He is inviting us to take on the identity He has for us so that we can fulfill our primary purpose of loving Him with all of our beings.

LIVE UP TO THE CALLING

God is inviting us to respond to His love and take on the identity He has for us. He names us "His Workmanship," "New Creation," "Disciple of Jesus," "Child of God," "Heir of God," and "More than Conqueror." He wants to submerge us in His identity and empower us through the Holy Spirit to take on these identities and make them who we are. However, there is an enemy who doesn't want us to believe the truth. The enemy's job is to keep us from seeing ourselves as God sees us. He has blinded many of us today from the truth by getting us to believe the lies that we are not beautiful, that we are in the wrong body, that we are the wrong gender, that we have to mutilate our bodies in order to feel better. He wants us to believe that we aren't qualified because of our past mistakes, current struggles, or that we are too young or too old, not rich enough, or too poor. He wants us to doubt what God says about us.

Unfortunately, many have fallen susceptible to these lies, believing them, and have rejected who God has made them to be. They look for ways to find happiness, trying to find hope and purpose in their old identities, and never growing to become who God has called us to be. Even as followers of Jesus, we sometimes go through life not knowing the truth of God's purpose for our lives. We go through life blind to our potential without even realizing it.

For some, this is just because they don't know any better. They've never been discipled or taught to go further in their relationship with Jesus. You'll never become who you're supposed to be if you don't know there is more.

Scripture says in Hosea that God's people perish because of a lack of knowledge (Hosea 4:6). While this passage is speaking more of a rejection of the truth by His people, this can also show that those who don't have the knowledge of their potential and purpose in Christ will never live full lives. They will never be like Him. Solomon shares a similar principle saying that people perish because of a lack of vision (Proverbs 29:18). Vision can only come when something is revealed. Truth must be revealed to be seen, then accepted. If the truth of our identity is not revealed to those who don't know it they will never be able to thrive as He designed us to.

Others have heard the truth their whole lives, but have never been able to believe and see it in themselves. Their own insecurities, imperfections, guilt, shame, or whatever lie they believe, have kept them blind to their own potential. Because of these lies, they live in a state of anxiety, depression, suicidal thoughts, or self-destructive habits that keep them from knowing their identity in Christ. Their identity is found more in the lie than the truth. As a result, they will never be like Christ.

Just like Jeremiah had to let go of his former identity of being young and not able to speak in order to take on his new identity as prophet, we must let go of all of the former identities and ways of doing things. Once we have let go God can give us the identity He wants us to have and empower the parts of us He wants to use to build His kingdom.

The Spirit of Wisdom and Revelation

I want to close out this section by praying the same prayer over you that Paul prays over the Ephesians in Ephesians 1.

"That the God of our Lord Jesus Christ, the Father of glory, may give to you the spirit of wisdom and revelation in the knowledge of Him, the eyes of your understanding being enlightened; that you may know what is the hope of His calling, what are the riches of the glory of His inheritance in the saints, and what is the exceeding greatness of His power toward us who believe, according to the working of His mighty power which He worked in Christ when He raised Him from the dead and seated Him at His right hand in the heavenly places, far above all principality and power and might and dominion, and every name that is named, not only in this age but also in that which is to come."

— *Ephesians* 1:17-21 (*NKJV*).

I pray that He would open your eyes to the plans He has for you and that you would realize that identity that He has given you to help you fulfill these plans.

Over the next few chapters, I will be talking about some practical ways to recognize the parts of our lives He wants to empower and use. Discovering these parts will help us to achieve our primary purpose of loving Him and loving others, taking on the identity He has for us, and helping us to fulfill our destiny.

Part 4 Find Your Purpose

"Love the LORD your God with all your heart, with all your soul, and with all your mind." and "Love your neighbor as yourself."

Matthew 22:37 and 39

Chapter 21

Your Part In God's Plan

Over the past few chapters I have talked about the discipleship process that we step into when we accept His invitation into love and begin following Him as His disciples. The discipleship process helps us to truly learn to love Him with all of our being. When we learn to love Him as Lord, we learn to obey His commandments and follow His teachings. When we learn to love Him as Father, we take on our identity as His sons and daughters. When we develop a deep and intimate relationship with Him we learn to love Him as Friend. As we learn to love Him, submerging ourselves into His identity, He gives us a new life in Christ.

However, there is something very important that we must remember. Following Jesus doesn't stop with just loving Him with all of our being. We must also love others. Without a love for others, we will never understand how to love God the way He wants us to. Also, loving God motivates us to love others because that's how we demonstrate that we love Him. Jesus tells us in John 13:35, "By this all will know that you are My disciples, if you have love for one

140

another" (NKJV). Only by loving others can we truly show that we love God and follow Him.

GOD'S PLAN

I have said over the course of this book so far that God has a plan for you. He has a plan in mind for you to thrive in every area of life and to love Him and love others. Something to remember though, is that His plan is not just for you. It's for everyone. In fact, His plan is for His entire creation. John 3:16, a very well-known verse, emphasizes this saying, "for God so loved the world that He gave His only begotten Son, that whoever believes in Him should not perish but have everlasting life" (NKJV). The word "world" that is used here is the Greek word *kosmos* which can be translated in a few ways. It can mean "the world or the universe" or the "inhabitants of the earth." [1] In John 3:17 Jesus continues His thought saying, "for God did not send His Son into the world to condemn the world, but that the world through Him might be saved" (NKJV). In other words, He loved His entire creation and the inhabitants of the world He created so much that He sent Jesus to save us from sin, redeeming His entire creation. This is the story of love and redemption that we are invited into. We have a part to play in this great plan of eternal salvation. We must love God and love people in order to accomplish His purpose for our lives.

Unfortunately, figuring out what part each of us are designed to play in God's plan is easier said than done. So many people misunderstand God's purpose out of ignorance or complacency. Many are disillusioned and discouraged because they can't figure out their place in life. Understanding God's invitation is the first step. Understanding our identity as we go through the discipleship process is an important next step. I talked about several of the identities that God gives us in the last section. He names us "New Creation," "Disciple of Jesus," "Child of God," "Heir of God," "More than Conqueror," and "His Workmanship." Understanding and allowing these identities to become who we are will help us to figure out what part God designed us to play in His story. As we take on these identities, our misconceptions about our purpose will shift. We will discover that we are created to "go" and "to do good works." This is how we love God and love people.

CREATED TO GO

God is inviting us to experience His love in a way that motivates us to accept His help and empowerment, giving us the ability to love Him and others perfectly so that all can know and love Him. When we accept this invitation, we are also accepting His invitation to go. Jesus tells us in Matthew 28:18-20, "all authority has been given to Me in heaven and on earth. Go therefore and make disciples of all the nations, baptizing them in the name of the Father and of the Son and of the Holy Spirit, teaching them to observe all things that I have commanded you" (NKJV).

The problem is in today's culture we have forgotten what it means to go. There are a few reasons people don't understand this "Great Commission." The first reason is because many believe that "going" is only for those "called into ministry." They misunderstand what calling is. The truth is this: everyone is "called into ministry." Jesus' invitation to follow Him is a "calling into ministry." The very definition of ministry is the act of ministering to someone or giving them service or aid. Every person who follows Christ is called to minister to the needs of others in whatever way they can.

For hundreds of years, the church has elevated the role of those in a church leadership role. Because of this, people believe that only those who are in church leadership roles are the ones who "have a calling." Priests, pastors, missionaries, and evangelists are the ones who preach the gospel, the ones who make disciples, and the ones who reach the lost. In the past, some denominations taught those who weren't in leadership roles that their pastors/priests were the voice of God and that they should depend solely on their spiritual leaders to learn the Bible and grow. In part, this was because of the lack of education for commoners. They had no way of learning to read the Bible because education was reserved only for clergy and nobility.

This elevation of church leadership, putting pastors on pedestals above normal congregants, has continued into today's Church society. There is still the mentality that it's up to church leaders and their families to do all the work of the ministry. Unfortunately, some church leaders have embraced this mentality, allowing unhealthy dependency on their teachings and leadership instead of challenging and discipling their congregations, teaching them how to grow, equipping them with the tools they need to be better witnesses, and then sending them out as ministers to the community. Because of this, Sunday church has become more about growing the church in numbers and keeping everyone happy and healthy than about growing the kingdom. People come to church to hear music and a message that makes them feel good, but don't leave changed and motivated to reach the lost. Research in 2021 by the Barna Group shows that only one in six, or 16 percent of American Christians read their Bibles every day of the week, increasing from 12 percent in 2020. 34 percent read the Bible once a week or less, and 50 percent read less than twice a year.[2] This is the biggest reason why there is so much misunderstanding about calling and purpose in our society today. Christians do not know Scripture.

CREATED TO DO GOOD WORKS

Some might ask "what part am I designed to play in God's plan?" They might say "I know I am called to go but I don't know what that means" or "Who or what am I called to go to?" Understanding the identity that we have as "His Workmanship" will help shed light on these questions. We are created by Him, designed for a purpose: to love God and love others. How do we accomplish this? By going and doing "good works, which God prepared beforehand that we should walk in them" (Ephesians 2:10). Something important to understand is that these acts of "good works" look different for each of us. God created each of us to be different from each other and each of us has a unique purpose that God designed us to achieve. For instance, God created me with a more emotional way of thinking. I am more emotional in how I make decisions and my talents are more creative. However, my wife, who is a nurse, has a more logical, scientific mind. God created her to understand things logically and practically and that's how she makes decisions. She's also very good at understanding things simply. As a nurse, she was designed to help people using her medical knowledge. Our differences in our personalities and ways of thinking show that our good works are very different as well. While I write, make music, and inspire people to grow through my creative talents, she helps people in practical ways. Something that is important to remember is that even though we are different, each of us is using those good works to love God and love people.

Just like the good works that my wife and I do are different, the different good works that each of us do to fulfill the purpose God has created us for will most likely look very different. The important thing to remember is that each of us has a part to play and that God wants to reveal how He wants to use you. He has a unique purpose that He designed you to achieve. You may not know what it is yet, but all it takes to find it is responding to His invitation to discipleship. Build a relationship with Him by seeking Him through prayer and reading scripture. Find out what He thinks and says about it. Find your identity. Growing in the identity He has for you as His disciple is the first step in the journey towards learning your purpose. The second step is to learn what good works He has called you to do by looking at what you already have to offer and asking how He wants to use you.

The story of how God called Jeremiah that I mentioned in the last section emphasizes this principle. Jeremiah had a mouth and a tongue that God created, giving him the natural ability to speak. He just wasn't confident in this ability. His way of thinking had to be transformed so that he could be used. He had to allow God to transform His identity into that of a prophet.

The same can be said of us. God has created us with hands, feet, mouth, etc. that can be used. We just have to think differently about ourselves in order to see that we can be used. God has given us the name "His Workmanship." We have been created to do good works with what God has given us. What are some things that you already have that God can use?

Chapter 22

Be Yourself

God wants to use us to grow His kingdom. He has a part for you to play in His plan. If you've been trying to figure out your destiny, find out what part He wants you to play. Playing your part in growing His kingdom will help you to fulfill the main purpose that He created you for, to love Him with everything that you are and to love others as yourself.

Here's the thing that is so great about this principle: God wants to use us no matter if we're qualified or not. So many people miss the fact that God can use them just as they are and that keeps them from performing the good works He has designed them to do. They compare themselves to people who have natural ministry gifts and assume that they lack the necessary talents and giftings to make disciples. However, when God chooses you, He doesn't expect you to become a different person than you are. He just wants you to love and follow Him. He will equip you to be the best version of yourself that you can be as you follow Him. So how does He equip us to be more like Him to grow His kingdom? Let me answer this question with two questions. What are your passions that drive you? What are your talents?

In counseling and pastoring young followers of Jesus through the years, I have asked these questions a lot. I am always shocked with how many respond that they don't know. They have no idea what their own passions and dreams are. They aren't able to recognize their own God-given talents and abilities. This shows a lack of self-aware-ness and self-confidence in today's society.

If we want God to create new life and purpose inside of us, we must realize who we are and be aware of what poten-tial we have, as well as our limitations. When we recognize who we are we learn to recognize our need for Him. It's when we learn of our lack of vision or just how self-absorbed our vision and dreams are that we can turn to Him to give us His dreams. When we learn to be aware of just how limited our own abilities are to achieve those dreams, we can turn to Him to transform us into the people He wants us to be.

However, God wants to use us just as we are. He is not trying to change us into different people, just better equipped, more confident, more aware, and purer versions of ourselves. An invitation to build His kingdom by obeying the call to go and do good works is an invitation to BE YOURSELF as you follow Him. Just follow Him joyfully and wholeheartedly and let Him worry about transforming you into the person who looks like Him. He will build His own kingdom through you as you continue along the journey of discipleship that you say yes to.

In my last book, I talked about how God leads us through seasons of growth that shape our character and make us more like Christ. God is not calling us to wait to GO until we are equipped, He's inviting us to GO just as we are and let Him use us to build His kingdom by doing good works. This is how we love Him and love others. He will transform us into the perfect versions of ourselves that He wants us to be. Versions who still have the same God-given personalities and talents, but who look like Him, act like Him, and talk like Him because we follow Him.

NATURAL GIFTS

So let me ask these questions again now that we understand what calling is a little better. "What are the passions that drive you?" "What are your talents?" The reason I ask these questions is this: the passions that we have are what drive us to accomplish a goal. Some people have a passion for exercise. That passion pushes them to go to the gym every day. I personally couldn't care less about exercise, but I have a passion for playing music. That passion pushes me to try my best to be the best I can be.

Whatever passions we might have that push us to accomplish something, change and grow over time as we follow Christ. When we learn to be like Him, He instills His passions for the lost, broken, and hurting inside of us. He then takes who we are and the natural talents that He has given us and uses us to grow His kingdom.

We also have talents that allow us to achieve our goals. These natural talents are part of who we are. I'll use my passion for music as an example. God has taken this passion and grown it, giving me the talents that I need to do what I'm passionate about well. He has given me the ability to use music to glorify Him. I wasn't always talented at music. However, when He called me to be a worship leader, He started developing my musical ability. Twenty years of experience later, I can now play drums, guitar, piano, and I can sing. He gave me a passion to see people enter His presence and equipped me with the talent to fulfill the purpose He had for my life. As I have been obedient, my musical talent has grown. The passion has grown as well. I love seeing people encounter Him and their lives be changed as I lead them into His presence through music. There is no greater calling than to use my talents to build His kingdom and see lives be changed. What about you? What are your passions and abilities?

As I said before, there have been some people who, when asked what their passions and talents are, respond, "I don't know." They don't know what they are passionate about or what their giftings are. Some of you who are reading this might fit this description. I want to challenge you to figure this out if you want to learn the part that God has for you in His kingdom. I would also encourage you to not overthink it. Some of you might have natural talents that you might not be aware of.

GROWING THE KINGDOM

We, as a society, elevate certain talents above others. Coming from a Pentecostal background, I have seen people who have certain spiritual gifts celebrated more than others who don't. In our American society we see that celebrities who have an acting or musical career are celebrated more than anyone else. They're our "idols." However, it's important to understand that in God's kingdom, no gift is more important than another. We all have our part to play in the Kingdom of God. He wants to use you no matter what your talent is. Figure out what drives you and what your giftings are and use them to grow His kingdom.

Let me give you an example from scripture. Paul gives this challenge in Romans 12:4-8,

> "For as we have many members in one body, but all the members do not have the same function, so we, being many, are one body in Christ, and individually members of one another. Having then gifts differing according to the grace that is given to us, let us use them: if prophecy, let us prophecy in proportion to our faith; or ministry, let us use it in our ministering; he who teaches, in teaching; he who exhorts, in exhortation; he who gives, with liberality; he who leads, with diligence; he who shows mercy, with cheerfulness" (NKJV).

Think about what Paul is saying. We are members of a body. Just like each part of our natural body has a purpose, we each have a purpose and calling that God is inviting us to achieve that will help the body function properly. If we aren't answering this invitation and performing that purpose, the body stops functioning properly. Paul lists a few giftings to emphasize this. Some of you might have one of these talents and not even realize it. Teachers should teach, givers should give, encouragers should encourage, prophets should prophecy, etc.

I'll add a few to this list. People who love babies or children can be in the nursery or children's ministry. Someone who loves landscaping and is good at it can use that talent and passion to serve the church and grow the kingdom. Someone who is a plumber can plumb toilets for the Kingdom of God.

Knowledge about something is also a gift that God is inviting you to use to grow His kingdom. Someone who is a doctor should realize that their knowledge of medicine is given to them by God to heal people. A lawyer or politician should use their knowledge of the law to grow the Kingdom.

Here's an overlooked one. If God has given you children to parent, raise them up well to be followers of Jesus. Parenting is a gift and ability given by God to grow His kingdom. We need to view it as such. Same thing with being an aunt or uncle. Being an aunt or an uncle is a gift from God that He wants to use to build His kingdom when we use it to disciple our nieces and nephews, teaching them about the ways of Jesus. I love to see how Jesus works in my nieces' and nephews' lives. I remember a time when my oldest nephew went to church with me when he was two or three years old. He was standing at the altar with my sister lifting up his hands to worship Jesus as I led worship. He wouldn't have known about Jesus if it wasn't for my family teaching Him about Jesus. There was another time when my nieces and nephew came over to help me redo the flower bed at our house. We had a thirty-minute-long conversation about spiritual things where they would ask me questions and I would do my best to answer them in a way they could understand. This role I have in their lives as their uncle is such a gift from God that, if used properly, will have an eternal impact on their lives. The same can be said of you whether you be a parent, aunt or uncle, or close family friend. God wants to use you to influence the kids in your lives who are close to you.

The list of gifts that God gives us can go on and on. There are lots of talents and passions that God wants to use use. Find yours and use it to grow His Kingdom. Respond to this invitation and call that God is extending to you.

In fact, every ability that we have is a gift and talent given to us by God to grow His kingdom. For instance, all of us breathe. Here's an idea for you to think about. Your breath is a gift from God that can be used to grow His king-dom. Our natural ability to move our fingers is a gift from God that can be used in some way. Your ability to smile is a gift from God to be used. You just have to figure out how you can use these abilities to help build His Kingdom. Get creative. Paul says in 1 Corinthians 10 that everything we do, we do for the glory of God. Yes, he's talking about what things are lawful and unlawful to do as Christians in this passage, but it still applies to this principle. We are invited to use whatever abilities we have been given by God for His glory and to grow His kingdom. Let us all respond willingly and joyfully to this invitation.

I'll use myself again to illustrate this principle. Like I said in the beginning of this chapter, I'm a musician and writer. I also am the worship director at my church. This is part of my identity. As a musician, I use my hands to play guitar and my mouth to sing. As an author I write thoughts in a way to help people learn more. However, before God called me to take on these identities I was like Jeremiah. I wasn't confident in my abilities and didn't feel like I was ready to accomplish the purpose of a pastor and worship leader that God called me to. I was very shy and was extremely scared to speak in public. But I knew God had called me, so I had to let Him transform my identity as a shy teenager into someone who was confident in who God had called me to be. I had to realize that He had given me the ability to do the things He has called me to do. I am His workmanship created with everything I need to do the good works He has designed for me to do. I have hands and a mouth that can be used, and He has called me to use them to build His kingdom. When I said yes to this calling, like Jeremiah, He transformed me into a strong, confident person who has been given the talent to do what God has called me to do. I might struggle sometimes with speaking properly, but it's more to do with excitement and talking too fast rather than fear now.

From Fishermen to Fishers of Men

You might be one of those people who think that you are unqualified to be used by God to do good works. What these people fail to realize is that everyone who God called in the Bible didn't start out in ministry. They started out as regular, average people who were mostly uneducated, messed up people. Let's take a look at the careers of the disciples who were with Jesus before they were called to follow Him:

Disciple	Career before Christ
Peter	fisherman
Andrew	fisherman
James son of Zebedee	fisherman
John son of Zebedee	fisherman
Phillip	fisherman

Bartholomew	Scholar, possibly a noble
Thomas	unknown career
Matthew	Tax collector
James son of Alphaeus	unknown
Thaddeus/ Jude	Unknown career, was a Nationalist
Simon the Zealot	Unknown career, was a zealot
Judas Iscariot	Unknown, possibly treasurer

As we see from this chart, Jesus called a variety of people. Most were uneducated fishermen from Galilee. Those who were educated came from careers that were considered lowly and corrupt, like tax collectors. Some were zealots, fighting against the Roman rule in Israel. While still young, possibly teenagers, according to scholars, they were old enough to have been working in their respective careers for a while.

Shepherd to King

King David, the greatest King in Israel's history, ancestor of Jesus, and a man who was known as a "man after God's own heart" was a shepherd before he became king. In those times, the duty of shepherding the flock was given to the youngest of the family while the older ones handled the more important tasks. When he was anointed as king, he wasn't the most popular or the strongest son of Jesse. He was the youngest and had the least important role of the family. But God still chose him to be king because he had a heart after God.

GOD INVITES ALL

We see from these examples that God doesn't look at status and ability when He chooses us. He chooses those who love Him and will give Him the glory because they know they can't do it without Him. He uses people from every career, background, with different abilities and potential, and with all kinds of weaknesses. He chooses men and women, people of every color, and people from every ethnic group, race and nationality. None are disqualified. All are invited to follow Him, and all are commanded to go and make disciples by doing good works that God created them to do.

Remember Jeremiah? Jeremiah wasn't qualified, but God still called him to be a prophet and empowered him to do what He designed him to do. If God were to do something similar with me as He did with Jeremiah, He probably would grab my hands and say something like "I have anointed your hands to play skillfully and given you the identity of pastor to help others experience who I am and grow. I have given you the words to write and songs to sing so that you can lead others into my presence so that they can find freedom and experience transformation." What is God saying to you? What is already in you that God wants to use?

If you are a doctor, He might grab your hands or put His hands on your head and say, "I have given you the knowledge and skills you need to heal the sick and see them recover. I have given you the identity of anointed doctor who heals in my Name. Go and grow my kingdom with this knowledge." If you are a lawyer, He might say, "I have given you the knowledge and voice to stand up for those who have no voice, protect the innocent, and be my justice to the wicked." If you are an athlete, He might touch your hands or feet and say, "I have given you the skills that you need to be a light where I have placed you. Be my hands and feet and lead others to me through your example." God wants to redeem, cleanse, and empower the parts of you that you already have so that you can use them to accomplish His plan for your life. For some like the disciples, it might be your career that helps you understand your God-given purpose. For others like me, it might be your natural passions and talents.

I hope you see where I'm going with this. He is the one who invites us to follow Him and equips us with what we need to accomplish His purpose. He wants to wake us up to this truth so that we can take on the identity that He has for us.

Chapter 23

Partnership With God

God is inviting all of His followers to play a part in His grand design to build His kingdom. We each have natural abilities and passions that He created and gave us to help us to accomplish the purpose and goals He has for us. But what if we don't have the necessary abilities to do what He calls us to do? Maybe the reality is that even though you have the confidence to do what God calls us to do, you might lack the knowledge or skill set. Like Jeremiah you might be called to be a prophet, but can't speak.

Maybe you are like so many in the Bible and aren't consistent with your relationship with Jesus, constantly falling into sin. Unfortunately, because of our sin nature and limited ability this is the case for all of us. Even though we might follow Jesus and gain maturity, we will always fall short in some ways. The reality is we can't accomplish the purpose God has for us on our own. We are too weak and limited. No matter how hard we try to love God and others well by doing good works we will always fail and fall short in some way.

However, even though we change and are fallible, God's plan to use us as we love Him and love others never changes. Even when we don't have the ability or are too weak to accomplish the purpose He has for us, He can step in and give us what we need to achieve the plan. He takes into account our weaknesses and failures. He can still use us when we are weak if we submit to His leadership. In fact, He uses our weakness to bring Himself glory. 2 Corinthians 12:9 emphasizes this when God tells Paul and us, "My grace is sufficient for you, for My strength is made perfect in weakness" (NKJV). He wants to get the glory from our lives when we follow Him. But, He also knows that we can't bring Him glory as we are. We can't possibly consistently love Him and love others all of the time without failing in some way. His plan for us is a partnership with Him where He does all of the work through us even when we are weak and fail. When we are weak and don't have the ability to do what He calls us to do, He steps in and helps us when we let Him, empowering us to do the task He's created us for. There are plenty of instances in Scripture where this happens. Let's take a look at some of these examples:

Abraham

Abraham was a friend of God, called to be the father of many nations. He was an example to us of what faith in God looks like. However, he messed up several times. He was a liar, lying in several instances in Scripture saying that Sarah was his sister instead of his wife out of fear. He also was impatient, taking the matter of having a child into his own hands by having sex with Hagar, his wife's servant, instead of waiting for God's perfect timing. He didn't trust God in any of these instances. He didn't have what it took to remain completely faithful in God's perfect plan. But, God still counted him as a friend because of his relationship with Him. He still achieved the purpose God had for him, because even during the times that he was weak, he remained faithful and depended on God to help him. God used his moments of weakness, turning them around for His glory when Abraham repented and chose to continue down the path that God had for him. Because of this relationship and dependance on God, Abraham is known as the father of our faith and is one of the heroes of faith listed in Hebrews 11.

David

David was another who had a great call on his life, but lacked the ability to be consistently faithful to God's commands. We see in Scripture that he messed up several times. He committed adultery and murder when he had sex with Bathsheba and then had her husband murdered so that he could marry her. He had multiple wives, some who were not the wisest choices, made because of his own lustful passions. He made several other mistakes during several periods of his rule that jeopardized the kingdom as well as his relationship with God. However, David always turned back to God, repented, and got back on the path of right-eousness that God had designed for him. Because of his dependance on God in spite of his failures, today we know him as a man after God's own heart and the ancestor of Jesus.

Peter

Peter was another who had to have help to become who

God had created him to be. Peter was one of the twelve chosen by Jesus to follow Him as His disciples. He was taught the ways of the Kingdom of God by Jesus Himself. He had a lot going for him. However, we see several things about Peter that showed that he needed some help. He wasn't the wisest of the disciples, always doing and saying things without thinking such as correcting Jesus, trying to convince Him that He didn't have to die in Matthew 16:23 and cutting the man's ear off in anger when Jesus was arrested. He also was easily distracted from Jesus by fear, such as when he began to sink when Jesus called him to walk on the water in Matthew 14 and when he denied Jesus three times in Matthew 26. However, with all of his character flaws we know that Peter loved Jesus. He just needed some help becoming who God had created him to be.

When We can't HE CAN

From the examples of all of these heroes of the faith we see one truth: even if we follow Jesus, we can't fully become who God has created us to be on our own. We will always lack something that holds us back. We need His help. Thankfully His plan and design for our lives includes His help. When we can't do it, He steps in and takes over if we allow Him to, helping us to achieve the purpose He designed for us. This is the partnership that we need to become who He has called us to be and achieve the purpose that He has designed us for. As part of this partnership, He sends the help that we need in the form of His Holy Spirit. The Holy Spirit is our Helper. He is also the One who equips us and empowers us to be the disciple that Jesus wants us to be (Acts 1:8). Without Him we cannot possibly accomplish what we have been designed to do. When we accept His invitation to respond to His love by becoming His disciples, the Holy Spirit fills us and begins the work of transformation inside of us. He begins teaching us how to live our lives as He has created us to, empowering us, and equipping us with the tools we need to accomplish the purpose He has for us.

Let's look at the examples of Jeremiah and Peter that I have used over the last few chapters to better understand this principle. Jeremiah had a weakness that inhibited him from becoming a prophet. He couldn't speak well. He needed God's help and empowerment to be able to speak the words that God wanted him to speak. We see that God touched Jeremiah's mouth saying that He was putting His words in His mouth. We see later in Jeremiah 20:9 that these words that God had given Jeremiah were "like a burning fire" shut up in Jeremiah's bones that he couldn't contain. As we see throughout the rest of Jeremiah, he goes to the nations and proclaims God's prophetic message. God's words, given to Him by His Spirit, who stepped in and equipped him with what he needed to overcome his weakness, were what transformed and empowered Jeremiah to become the prophet God had designed Him to be.

The Holy Spirit does the same thing for us today. Jesus tells His disciples in Luke 12:11-12, "Now when they bring you to the synagogues and magistrates and authorities, do not worry about how or what you should answer, or what you should say. For the Holy Spirit will teach you in that very hour what you ought to say" (NKJV). When God gives us a task to do and something to say to those in our lives, the Holy Spirit will give us the words to say, when we are willing to be used.

Peter is another example of what happens when God steps in to give us what we lack. As I mentioned earlier,

Peter was brash and emotional, not thinking before he spoke and acted, and was full of fear that kept him from living up to the potential in Jesus that he had. We see this demonstrated in the accounts when he denied Jesus three times (Matthew 26:69-75, Mark 14: 66-72, Luke 22:55-62, John 18:16-27). However, we see in Acts chapter 2 something that changed Peter and gave him what he needed to overcome his limitations and weaknesses. Acts 2:1-4 describes what happened:

> "When the Day of Pentecost had fully come, they were all with one accord in one place. And suddenly there came a sound from heaven, as of a rushing mighty wind, and it filled the whole house where they were sitting. Then there appeared to them divided tongues, as of fire, and one sat upon each of them. And they were all filled with the Holy Spirit and began to speak with other tongues, as the Spirit gave them utterance" (NKJV).

This was the moment that the Holy Spirit came and rested on those who followed Jesus, empowering them to be "better witnesses" as Jesus had promised in Acts 1:8. All who were in the area were confused trying to figure out what was going on. However, Peter stood up and preached to everyone, explaining that this was the promise made by God in Joel 2 and saying that Jesus was the promised Messiah. What's amazing is that this was less than two months from when he denied Jesus three times! With the Holy Spirit's help, Peter could accomplish the task that Jesus had given him before His ascension. He asked Peter three times in John 21 saying "Peter, do you love me?" to which Peter replied all three times, "Yes Lord you know I love you." Peter's reply is the same that ours would be, but

Peter had proven only days before that he was incapable of loving Jesus perfectly, denying Him three times. However, it was at this moment that Jesus gave Peter a second chance for him to prove his love. He said to Peter the first time, "feed my lambs," the second time, "tend my sheep," and the last time "feed my sheep." On the day of Pentecost, we see Peter take advantage of this second chance, feeding the thousands of people who were there the truth about who Jesus was. This was Peter's demonstration that with help, he could indeed love Jesus the way He wanted him to by feeding the sheep. With the help of the Holy Spirit's empowerment Peter went from someone bound by fear to someone who could declare boldly in front of thousands of people that Jesus was God and that they needed to follow Him.

The Holy Spirit wants to do the same for us today, empowering all of us who are flawed and incapable of loving Jesus with everything that we are, giving us the things we need to feed the sheep in our lives. He wants to take what is broken inside of us, redeeming it, and fixing it so that we can be used. He wants to give us the power that we need to fulfill the purpose He created us to achieve, to love Him and love others. All we need to do is accept His invitation and the second chances that He gives us just like Peter did.

Chapter 24

The Supernatural

Something else that's an amazing part of our partnership with God is that He invites us into a supernatural life when we respond to His invitation to become His disciples. This is an important element of our destiny and purpose that many don't take advantage of. As heirs of God, we have been given the same power and authority that Jesus had when He walked on earth. Paul tells us in Romans 8:11 that the same power that raised Jesus from the dead lives inside of us. This power comes from the person of the Holy Spirit. The Holy Spirit comes to live in us when we declare Jesus as Lord and become His disciples. When we submit to His leadership, allowing Him to fill us in every area of our lives, the Holy Spirit gives us the power to live supernatural lives with His help, doing good works that are beyond our natural human ability. We see this supernatural lifestyle all throughout the book of Acts. The apostles performed many signs, wonders, and miracles and many souls were added to the church daily, fulfilling what Jesus had promised when He said that those who follow Him would heal the sick, cast out demons, raise the dead, and do other signs, wonders, and miracles (Mark 16:17-18, Matthew 10:8).

How many of you have performed or seen a sign, wonder, or miracle? How many of you have seen sick people healed, the lame walk, or the blind see? How many of you have seen demons being cast out or dead people being raised from the dead by those who believe? For the early church these things were normal because they accepted God's invitation into a supernatural lifestyle of power and authority with the help of the Holy Spirit.

Here's the thing that the church today has either forgotten, doesn't understand, or doesn't take advantage of because of complacency or fear: the Holy Spirit wants to empower us to live the same supernatural lifestyle that the early church did. He wants to give us the gifts of the Spirit that help us walk in the promise of God and in the identity as His heirs, operating in supernatural power and authority.

THE GIFTS OF THE SPIRIT

In 1 Corinthians 12 Paul teaches the church in Corinth about these gifts that every believer has access to when they accept the Holy Spirit's invitation to empowerment. He states

> "there are diversities of gifts, but the same Spirit. There are differences of ministries, but the same Lord. And there are diversities of activities, but it is the same God who works all in all. But the manifestation of the Spirit is given to each one for the profit of all: for to one is given the word of wisdom through the Spirit, to another the word of knowledge through the same Spirit, to another

166

faith by the same Spirit, to another gifts of healings by the same Spirit, to another the working of miracles, to another prophecy, to another discerning of spirits, to another different kinds of tongues, to another the interpretation of tongues. But one and the same Spirit works all these things, distributing to each one individually as He wills" (NKJV).

These gifts are meant to enhance our ministries and the "good works" that we naturally do already, allowing us to operate beyond ourselves to accomplish the purpose that God has for us.

Spoken Gifts

Words of knowledge, wisdom, tongues and the necessary interpretation, and prophetic words are all messages given by the Holy Spirit to an individual to speak directly to the church or a person who needs it. These words are supernatural utterances meant to give encouragement, reveal the need for repentance of sin, or to warn the church. It's important to note that these messages are beyond the speaker's natural ability and understanding. It is a message that is supernaturally spoken from the Holy Spirit, relayed through the person He has given the gift to. We see these gifts operated in several instances in the early church such as when Peter revealed the truth of Ananias and Sapphira's lie in Acts chapter 5. Peter did not know that they were lying until the Holy Spirit revealed it supernaturally. The prophets of the Old Testament are also examples of how the Holy Spirit speaks supernaturally through people using the gift of prophecy. The prophecies were given to the prophets by the Holy Spirit when the nation needed to be rebuked or encouraged by God. The prophets were just ordinary people given an extraordinary purpose and equipped with what they needed to achieve that purpose.

Faith

Faith is another gift of the Spirit that the Holy Spirit gives to His people. We all have a natural measure of faith. In some this measure is very small, others it's larger. However, a partnership with the Holy Spirit allows Him to give us more faith when we ask for it. This supernatural gift of faith allows us to persevere in trials, trust in Him to move through us when we step out in obedience to Him, and to see miracles occur when we believe in and follow Him. Faith gives us a greater expectation of supernatural things to happen because we walk with Jesus. However, it takes a partnership with the Holy Spirit for this kind of faith to grow inside of us.

Healing and Miracles

The gifts of healings and working of miracles are the supernatural gifts of the Holy Spirit that allow us to operate in His power and authority. The miracles and healing that we see in the book of Acts are all examples of this gift being used by the early church. Acts 2 illustrates this principle clearly. Verse 43 clearly states that the apostles performed many wonders and signs. Every chapter that follows in the book of Acts talks about something supernatural that occurs when those who believed were around. The sick were healed, the dead were raised, the blind could see, and the lame could walk because of their partnership with the Holy Spirit. It wasn't their power that achieved these things, but the power that came from the Holy Spirit who dwelled within them. When we follow the Holy Spirit and allow Him to use us we can walk in the same power.

Discerning of spirits

Discerning of spirits is the last gift that I haven't talked about yet. Discernment is a necessary part of our lives as followers of Jesus. There are a lot of "truths" out there that we need to recognize aren't from God. The Holy Spirit is the one who gives us this discernment and is how we distinguish what is from God and what isn't. Discernment is how He leads and directs our steps. This means that this gift can only come from an active relationship with the Holy Spirit. We must learn to listen to His voice speaking and leading us. There are times where we need His discernment to recognize when He wants us to speak or not to speak, where to go, and what to do. The story of Paul and the slave girl who practiced divinity in Acts 16 is the perfect example from Scripture that illustrates this gift. The slave girl was following them shouting, "These men are the servants of the Most High God, who proclaim to us the way of salvation." Taken at face value this might not seem like a bad thing because this was the truth. They were indeed servants of the Most High God and were there to lead them to salvation. However, through the discernment of the Holy Spirit, Paul recognized that the girl was being used by a demon to speak these things and was able to cast the demon out, setting her free. Paul recognized with the help of the Holy Spirit that this girl was bound by evil and that she needed to be free. When we have discernment, we can see through the deception of the enemy, recognizing that what seems to be good and true isn't from God and therefore a deception that will bring our destruction. It is extremely important to remember that discernment is a supernatural gift that can only come from an active relationship with the Holy Spirit.

WE ALL HAVE ACCESS

Something that is important to realize about these gifts is that the Holy Spirit still wants to give them to us today. There are those that believe that the gifts of the Spirit were just for the twelve apostles and weren't given anymore after they died. This simply isn't accurate. The testimony of Paul himself clearly disproves this. He wasn't among the twelve original apostles, becoming a follower of Jesus years later. He also clearly operated in the gifts of the Spirit. The gifts were also clearly used by others in the book of Acts who weren't part of the twelve original apostles in the early church. If you don't believe me then just read the book of Acts.

There is also documentation that these gifts have been used throughout history since. Several of the Catholic saints were known to have been used to perform miracles as they followed Jesus and preached the gospel. There are denominations today that actively see the gifts of the Spirit occurring in their church services. I was raised in a church that believed in the gifts of the Spirit and I have seen crazy supernatural things happen throughout my life. My own brother was born with a busted eardrum and was deaf in his right ear for twenty-one years until his pastor prayed for him at a New Year's Eve church service, and he was healed! There are many more testimonies of God doing things like this that I have been a part of myself! There was one specific time when I worked for a campus ministry called Chi Alpha where I challenged a group of college students to believe for healing to occur when they prayed. In the middle of Washington D.C. on a sidewalk on our way to the Lincoln Memorial these students and I prayed for another student who had worn hearing aids for most of her life. She was healed and was able to take her hearing aids out for the first time in years!

You can't tell me that God doesn't move in these ways anymore. I have seen too many miracles to believe otherwise. There is too much evidence today pointing to the truth that God is still using people to do supernatural things to build His kingdom.

God wants to use us in these ways to grow His kingdom. He wants to give His people the gifts of words of wisdom, knowledge, prophecy, tongues, interpretations of tongues, healing, miracles, discernment, and faith as supernatural ways to make disciples. These gifts are the "good works" that He created us to perform when we accept His invitation to partner with Him, taking on the identity He has for us. These gifts are given freely to all who believe.

You might be wondering how can I get these gifts? The answer is simply this: "seek first the kingdom of God and His righteousness, and all these things shall be added to you" (Matthew 6:33, NKJV). What this means is when we "seek His kingdom and righteousness" we seek to understand what His kingdom is all about. What part do we play in His kingdom? What things do we need to accomplish our part in His kingdom? What do we need to be righteous? We also learn to seek Him as King of the kingdom and His identity for us. As we discover Him, He reveals Himself, filling our lives with the knowledge of who He is and what His plans are. The gifts of the Spirit are part of His plan and design for all believers. So, if we seek our place in His kingdom we also need to "earnestly desire the best gifts" as

Benton J. Ward

Paul says in 1 Corinthians 12:31. All of the gifts of the Spirit help us do the "good works which God prepared beforehand that we should walk in them" (Ephesians, 2:10 NKJV), fulfilling the purpose that God has for us to love Him and love others.

Chapter 25

Love Others

'Whom shall I send, and who will go for Us?' Then I said, 'Here am I! Send me'"

— Isaiah 6:1-8 (NKJV).

God has invited us to experience His love in a way that motivates us to love Him back and to love others. We love others by going and doing the good works He has designed us to do. He wants to send us to people who don't know Him in order to help them experience His love. This is how we love others. Just like He did with Isaiah, He is asking "who will go?" In other words, He's asking "who will love Me and love others enough to go." Because we love God and love people our response should be like Isaiah's "Here I am! Send me!"

However, God's calling to go and do good works isn't the same for everyone. We are all designed to be different and have different good works that we have each been uniquely designed to do. Some might be called to be in church leadership roles, designed to be apostles, prophets, evangelists, pastors, and teachers who are responsible for "the equipping of the saints for the work of ministry, for the edifying of the body of Christ" as Paul teaches in Ephesians 4:11-12.

Some of us might not be called to be one of these who equip the church, but have just as important of a purpose to fulfill. After all, God puts certain natural passions and abilities inside of us that He wants to use. If you have a passion for children and an ability to love children well by teaching them, then God most likely has designed you to go and love children, helping them to experience His love. If you have a passion and talent for business, then God wants you to use your business to grow His kingdom. If you have a passion for giving and helping people with financial needs, then God wants you to go make disciples by giving to help the poor. The list goes on.

Whatever the case may be, God wants you to go and make disciples. Go and use the gifts and passions that God has created within you to love others. God also wants to empower you to live a supernatural life. Partner with the Holy Spirit who lives inside of you and wants to make you into the best version of yourself. Ask Him to give you the gifts of the Spirit that will enable you to do more "good works" through His power to grow His kingdom.

Also, if you don't know what your talents and passions are or don't feel like you have any, then I would encourage you to ask God to give you ideas of how you can love others. Ask Him what good works He has designed you for. Think about the things that I talked about earlier. What do you like to do? Do you like to help people? Do you like children? Do you like to give? Do you like to build things? I'm sure you can think of some things. Write down what motivates you the most and think about how you can use them to accomplish the purpose that God has for you

As you discover what good works you were designed for then the next step is to allow God to plant you in a community where you can do these good works. This is how you achieve your purpose of loving Him and loving others well.

Part 5 The Kingdom

"But seek first the kingdom of God and His righteousness, and all these things shall be added to you."

Matthew 6:33

Chapter 26

Community

Over the last few chapters I introduced the principle of loving others. Loving others is the result of experiencing God's love, letting it motivate us to become His disciples, learning to love Him the way He wants us to. We can't love God with all our mind, soul, body, and strength without loving others. We love others by doing "good works which God prepared beforehand that we should walk in them." This is our identity and is how people know we are Jesus's disciples.

However, there is an important principle we must never forget if we are to achieve the purpose that God created and designed us for. Loving others like God loves them requires healthy, growing, and consistent relationships with other people. The relationships with people that you build that are healthy and growing are what make up your community. The definition of community "is a group of people living in the same place or having a particular characteristic in common." Having a community built of healthy relationships is a necessary part of being a disciple of Jesus.

I've mentioned throughout this book that I went

through a season where I experienced severe discontentment. I was a young adult's pastor at the time, but I was so focused on my future and finding my purpose that I didn't serve God well as a pastor. In fact, I was so discontent and frustrated that I lost all desire to build healthy relationships with anyone, including the young adults in my life group. This is not normal for me because I love to be around people and talk about Jesus, especially young adults and college students. Unfortunately, my own frustrations controlled me more during this season than I care to admit. It got to the point that during the third year of this season, which just happened to be during COVID, I did nothing to grow relationships and used COVID as an excuse to stay at home after work and watch Netflix or read a book. I didn't even try to consistently check up on anyone from my life group to see how they were doing. Because I neglected my purpose and my community, I spiraled further and further into discontentment.

Fortunately, there were two people who helped me to stay focused on my relationship with Jesus, even if I didn't try to grow my relationships with others. The first one was a friend who was like a second mom to me who was also a life coach and pastoral counselor. She allowed me to come over and vent all of the time, helping me to process things that I was experiencing and gave me wise advice. The second was my pastor. He was very patient with me, believing in my calling, and helping me to try to figure out my life. Both were patient with me and encouraged me as I went through this season. Thankfully, I allowed them to continue to pour into me instead of completely isolating myself, as others do when they experience challenging times.

With their help and encouragement, God showed me the answer to my problems. I needed to stop trying to do things my own way and learn to be His disciple again. I needed to rebuild my community and do life with people who also followed Him.

No matter where you are in your journey with Christ, no matter if you are an introvert or an extrovert, and no matter if you have sin in your life or not, you need other people who will follow Christ with you. Isolating ourselves is the worst thing we can do when we are going through trials and suffering. Isolation also keeps us from growth and maturity. Throughout the rest of this chapter, and over the course of the next few chapters, I want to talk about a few principles that will explain the need for community as we journey with Jesus. My hope is that these principles will help explain how building a healthy community helps us to love God with all of our being and love others as ourselves.

KINGDOM COMMUNITY

I mentioned in an earlier chapter that love is the breeding ground for transformation and growth. Love established and demonstrated in a community is the ground necessary for transformation to occur both in yourself and in others. Only through a life with others in community can we learn what purpose God has for us. Community is the place where we can truly accomplish that purpose.

God Himself establishes a community with those who follow Him. This community is called His Kingdom. When we accept His invitation to follow Him, we enter His Kingdom community. Jesus taught about God's Kingdom while He was on the earth. He used parables to teach principles that showed some different characteristics of God's Kingdom community.

Parable of the Mustard Seed (Matthew 13:31-32)

In the Parable of the Mustard Seed found in Matthew 13:31-32 Jesus teaches that the "kingdom of heaven is like a mustard seed." The mustard seed is one of the smallest tree seeds. However, even though it is small it grows into a large tree. This parable is important to remember because it shows us that God wants to use us no matter how small we might seem to be.

We can learn from this parable as we learn to love God and love people. There are times where we might feel insignificant, but as members of the Kingdom of God we have the potential to be places of rest and healing for those around us, just as the tree is a place of rest and a home for the birds. If we are available to be used where He plants us, He will use us to build His Kingdom community.

Parable of the Leaven (Matthew 13:33)

Jesus continues His teaching on the Kingdom of God with the Parable of the Leaven saying that "the kingdom of heaven is like leaven" (Matthew 13:33). Leaven is what is used in bread to make it rise. It only takes a small amount to change the entire loaf of bread. What Jesus is teaching us in this parable is this: even though there is only a little bit of leaven in the meal, it changes the chemistry of the entire meal until everything is leavened. The same can be said of those who follow Christ and have responded to the invitation to be a part of God's kingdom and do His will on the earth. Even though we might seem to be few, with His help and power we can transform the world around us into what He desires it to be. However, the point of leaven is that it is placed intentionally into dough to accomplish what it was designed to accomplish. Once placed it can change the chemical makeup of the bread. God places us intentionally into the world to change it from the inside out. We have to let ourselves be used where He places us to change the atmosphere of the city, friend group, school, etc. that we are in.

Parables of the Lost Sheep and the Lost Coin (Luke 15:1-10)

There are two more parables that demonstrate what those who make up His Kingdom community are like. The parable of the lost sheep and the parable of the lost coin found in Luke 15 demonstrate that Jesus would never give up on finding one lost soul, going as far as to leave the other sheep behind to search for the lost one. These parables teach us that there is value in what seems to be lost, hurt, and broken. If we accept His invitation to love God and love others, we are to love others just like Jesus, pursuing the lost until they are found. In order to represent His kingdom well and do His will on the earth we must do what He would do no matter what. He would leave the 99 sheep and search everywhere to find the one lost. If we can't see the lost, broken, and hurting with the same compassion and love, then we are not accepting His invitation to love others by going and doing good works, partnering with Him to grow His kingdom on the Earth.

INVITED INTO RELATIONSHIP

As I talked about in the last chapter, an invitation to love others requires us to go and do good works to make disciples. However, in order for us to make disciples there needs to be a healthy relationship built. These relationships make up your community. The parables that Jesus taught about the kingdom of God show that God invites us to build relationships and community both with Him and with others. When we have established those relationships with others, He wants to use us to change those we have built a relationship with and make them His disciples as well.

However, we must understand that there is a process to grow a relationship, both with God and with others. I talked about how to grow a relationship with God in the beginning of this book: we seek God and learn who He is through prayer and reading scripture. However, there is an important principle in relationship building that I want to talk about that applies to both our relationship with God and others. Building healthy relationships first requires a connection.

Chapter 27

Creating Connection

God wants us to love others. This is the second part of the primary purpose that He has designed us to achieve. The first part is to love Him. Loving others can only be done by allowing yourself to be planted into a community and developing relationships. However, in order for community relationships to be built, a connection must be established.

Connection is something that draws us to another person. Experiencing God's love is what establishes that connection with Him. When we experience His love, it causes us to want to know Him more. Establishing a connection with others is a little harder with other people than with God. Some people are just hard to love. People, especially those who don't follow Jesus, can be mean, rude, arrogant, angry, and bitter people. Some people have various types of personalities. Some love to spend time with others, some don't like others, preferring life on their own for various reasons making it hard to build a connection with. However, when we follow God, allowing Him to transform us and give us the identity He wants us to have, we begin to also experience a deep love for others. This love that can only come from God motivates us to build connection with them, no matter how unlovable they are or how much we don't want to because of our own personality.

In the last section, I talked about how we are to "go and make disciples of all the nations, baptizing them in the name of the Father and of the Son and of the Holy Spirit" (Matthew 28:19). As we go, we do the good works that we have been designed to do. There is something important that the modern church needs to remember. Going and doing good works is only a part of our purpose. We don't go and do good works for no reason. The reason we go and do good works is to help others become disciples of Jesus. This is how we grow God's kingdom. Doing good to help people is a good thing for sure but the world is full of "good" people that do good. The difference between us and the world is that we know Jesus, they don't. Our good works are full of Jesus's love and truth, theirs isn't. Their good works won't give anyone a hope for salvation or a bright future that goes beyond death into eternity, ours will. As followers of Jesus, our purpose is to make disciples by the good works we do as we go. The message of salvation, truth, and hope that is found in Jesus is what sets us apart from the world.

Since a disciple of Jesus is a lifelong student or apprentice of Jesus, making disciples requires being in someone's life long enough to help them become a lifelong disciple of Jesus. There is a method that Jesus used that we can follow. He didn't approach people and demand that they follow Him without first establishing some kind of connection. He first showed that He was someone worth following, demonstrating that He cared for them. The Son of God met them where they were, established a connection, and built a relationship with them. He ate with them, walked with them, talked with them, and met their needs. He related to them. He was intentional about not only being their Master but being their friend. This should be our discipleship model as we go and make disciples. We can never share the truth effectively with someone we don't first have a relationship with. Jesus models a few practical methods to help build connection with others.

Practical Method to Build Connection #1: FOOD

There is nothing more powerful in relationship building than when you share a meal together. In every culture, there is one way to a person's heart: food. The best way to invite a non-believer into your life, and insert yourself into theirs, is sharing a meal together. We see Jesus going to people's houses for dinner all the time. Zacchaeus, the "wee little man" in Luke 19:1-10, is the perfect example of this. Zacchaeus was a tax collector who was hated by the people because he cheated them constantly. But that all changed when Jesus came over for dinner. Zacchaeus experienced His love for him, and it moved him to repentance. His life was changed in a moment. The simple act of Jesus sharing a meal with him despite his mistakes was all it took for transformation to take place in Zacchaeus' life. He repaid all the money that he had stolen from people and gave his riches to the poor. Imagine if we did the same thing to the people in our lives. Imagine if someone had invited people like Hitler, Osama Bin Laden, or Jeffrey Dahmer to a meal and shared the gospel with them. Jesus would have. Their lives and the roles that they played in events in history would probably have turned out differently if someone had been like Jesus to them.

In the book of Acts, after the birth of the church on the day of Pentecost, we see that not only did the church grow in knowledge of who Jesus was, but they broke bread together daily. This shows the importance of building connections that lead to relationship and community in the body of Christ. It's through community and our love for one another that people know we are disciples of Jesus. Every person desires this same community. If you're looking for a way to grow your community utilize this method. Food is a very effective way to establish connection with others.

Practical Method to Build Connection #2: SERVING

Another method that Jesus used to build connection was by meeting needs wherever He went. Whether it was a sick person who needed healing, a woman caught in sin who needed forgiveness, someone who was depressed who needed encouragement, someone who was demon possessed needing freedom, etc., Jesus met their needs with love and compassion. He met our need for a savior by giving up His life. In other words, Jesus came to serve others. He tells His disciples in Mark 10:45, "For even the Son of Man did not come to be served, but to serve, and to give his life as a ransom for many" (NKJV). Serving and meeting others' needs helps establish a connection. We see in scripture that those who had their needs met by Jesus followed Him and proclaimed Him as Lord. When we serve out of compassion and love without expecting anything in return, we show others the same love and compassion that Jesus has for them. His love shown through our good works as we meet a need is what creates true connection that leads to lasting relationship and brings transformation.

Practical Method to Build Connection #3: STORIES

Another way that Jesus engaged the people was through stories. The parables He taught showed the people who He was and taught them about the Kingdom of God. All of us have stories to share as well. There is power in our stories, the testimonies of what God has done for us. Some of us might not feel that way about our stories, believing that since we don't have a radical testimony it wouldn't be worth mentioning. However, the fact that Jesus saved us from a life of sin and gave us what we need to be who He designed us to be is a story that speaks volumes about the truth, grace, and mercy of God. It doesn't matter if we've done terrible things in our past or if we grew up in church; Jesus still saved us and has transformed us. We should shout this truth from the rooftops and brag about Him every chance we get. He can and wants to do it for those who don't know Him as well. Just like the stories from the Bible help us learn how to be like Jesus and grow in faith and knowledge that He is good and faithful, so your stories of what God has done and can do can help those around you know Christ and experience freedom.

BE LIKE JESUS

All of these methods are excellent ways to build connection. However, until we develop a love for others just like Jesus did we will never be able to master the art of building connections with others like He did. It takes a heart that is transformed and understands the necessity of loving others to be able to build relationships that lead to disciples being made. It first takes us experiencing God for ourselves and encountering His love for us that transforms. When we accept His invitation to love Him and become His disciples He gives us a heart that is capable of loving others who might be unlovable. At the moment we experience Him and respond to His invitation into discipleship, we begin the journey of learning to be like Jesus so that we can love our neighbor as ourselves.

Chapter 28

Love Your Neighbor

Jesus is inviting us into a journey of love. He invites us to experience His love for us and to respond to it by becoming His disciples. When we become His disciples we start a lifelong journey of learning what it means to be His disciples, taking on the identity that He has for us. It is also a journey where we learn to love others like ourselves. Loving God and loving others are our primary purposes.

Loving others is hard sometimes though. Some people are unlovable. As part of the discipleship journey, God wants to transform our hearts so that we can love others like He loves them. Loving others starts with building a connection that leads to a healthy relationship where discipleship can occur. Today evangelism is the church term that we use to say that we are trying to reach the lost. Establishing a connection that can lead to discipleship is the main form of evangelism that we have.

Unfortunately, the church in the past few hundreds of years has lost this mindset. Instead of making disciples we have settled for making converts. Evangelism has become more about asking people if they "know Jesus." If they don't, we tell them that they need to get saved. We lead these people in a prayer called the "sinner's prayer" and then celebrate that they are "saved."

However, in a lot of cases, there is no discipleship that occurs after this salvation. After the brief encounter these souls are usually left alone and forgotten about. In these cases, they are converts, not disciples. True evangelism isn't about making converts. It's about building the necessary connection with someone that can lead to a continued relationship where discipleship can occur. Going to those in our lives and doing good works for them is just the first step in establishing a connection that results in a disciple making relationship. This is the first step in loving our neighbors as ourselves. Helping them become faithful disciples of Jesus is the second step.

WHO IS MY NEIGHBOR?

Before we go any further there is something I want to explain more. Jesus calls us to love our neighbors as ourselves. Understanding who your neighbor is will help you to understand your purpose more. I want to answer the questions I brought up in another chapter that a lot of people have: "Who is God sending me to?" "Where is God sending me?"

In the story where Jesus first summarized the first two greatest commandments "love the Lord your God with all your heart and with all your soul and with all your strength and with all your mind and, love your neighbor as yourself" (Luke 10:27, NKJV), the Pharisee that Jesus was talking to responded by asking this question "who is my neighbor?" (Luke 10:29, NKJV). Jesus responds by telling the Parable of the Good Samaritan. I'm not going to go in depth in this parable right now, but I want to point something out to us that will answer this question of who our God is sending us to as well as where. The story ended with a Samaritan who was considered by Jews to be the lowest of the low helping a Jewish man who had been beaten by robbers. At the end of the story Jesus asked the Pharisees who was the neighbor. The answer was "the one who had mercy on him" (Luke 10:37, NKJV)

The Lost

There are those in your life that need mercy. They need to experience God's love in a way that leads them to repentance and become followers of Jesus just like you. They might be beaten down by sin, broken by the challenges of life and need you to be the Good Samaritan in Jesus's story. Some might not appear to be broken, but their hearts are still a mess. Just like you and I are, they are in need of a Savior. In reality, every person in your life needs Jesus. They might be different from you, but they are still bound by sin, and are still walking in darkness. They have the same need of a savior as you do. The difference is you have been set free and can now see and hear while they are still blind and deaf. Jesus wants you to be the light that they see, and the voice of God that they hear. He wants to speak through you and shine His light into their darkness. How does He do that? The same way Jesus did. By building a connection that leads to a relationship where discipleship can occur.

In the World

Unfortunately, American Christianity has become a society that misrepresents what it means to be "in this world but not of this world." We have created our own Christian subculture. This is not necessarily a bad thing, but unfortunately, it has caused a mentality that says that in order to stay Christlike, we have to be separate from the world and avoid relationships with nonbelievers. I remember when I was a teenager being told at youth conferences and camps that we shouldn't hang out with sinful people because they would be a bad influence on us. While I think that is true to a certain extent because who we hang out with could have a negative influence on us, I don't believe that avoiding people who don't believe in Jesus altogether is the answer. This is the biggest reason the average Christian has a misunderstanding of what it means to "go and make disciples." We have separated ourselves from non-believers and created a culture that is completely separate from the world. Some homeschool their kids because they don't want them to experience the darkness of secular society and possibly become corrupt themselves. We encourage our high school seniors to go to Christian universities. I do want to stress that my intention is not to say that homeschooling and going to a Christian university is bad. There is nothing wrong with homeschooling and Christian universities. In fact, there are educational benefits to both. I got my masters in pastoral counseling through a Christian university. A few of my best friends were all homeschooled. My nieces and nephews are all being homeschooled and my sister in law is doing a great job making sure they understand Christian principles and the need to reach the lost.

However, we have to examine our motives for why we

choose to go those routes. Fear of our kids being corrupted by society is not a good reason. We need to trust Jesus with our children. If we teach our children to follow Jesus at a young age and set the example of what it means to be His disciple, as well as how to make disciples, we will see them do things that even the bravest adult wouldn't normally do. I've heard stories of young children under ten years old laying hands on the sick and seeing crazy miracles happen because they emulated their parents and listened to their teachings. If we shelter our children more than necessary, it actually harms them rather than helps them.

I also have another reason why I believe that students should be encouraged to go to secular schools, especially those who feel called into full time ministry. As a former missionary with Chi Alpha Campus Ministries and graduate from a secular campus, I admit I am biased and believe that everyone who follows Jesus should go to a secular university unless they want to go into a specific ministry field that requires a degree from a Christian seminary. I have a reason for this bias, though. There is an immense need for the gospel to be shared on college campuses. Students who feel a calling into ministry, but don't have a specific focus requiring a specific degree only taught by Christian universities, would benefit greatly from experiencing ministry firsthand. They would learn how to make disciples from experience and training, not just going to theology classes. Christian students have their faith tested constantly in a secular environment. They have to develop a strong relationship with Jesus and trust in Him in order to see His kingdom come on campus. While they do get great classes that teach theology and the theories of church leadership at Christian colleges, they don't get their faith, relationships with Christ, and knowledge of the Bible and who

He is tested and strengthened as much by going to a Christian university.

However, like I said before, I understand the benefits of going to a Christian university. I'm not bashing them, and believe they are great for believers to learn what Christianity is about, but I believe we should give students who grow up in church every option and explain the value. Only promoting Christian universities to high school students in our denominations limits what we can see God do to teach young people how to be like Him. There are also many other ministry education options that students can utilize while attending a secular university if they really want extra theology training.

PRACTICAL CHRISTIANITY

The point I am trying to make with saying all of that is this: we need to get out of our Christian bubbles. Staying in our Christian bubble is the reason why most Christians are given a bad name and mistrusted nowadays. There is a lot of truth being preached at people, but no relationships being built. This leads to mistrust and hatred towards Christians. Let me ask you this: would you listen to someone you didn't know personally telling you that you were going to hell? Or would you listen to someone who had a relationship with you telling you that they loved you and didn't want anything bad to happen to you? I would definitely be more inclined to listen to the second and ignore the first. The same is true of those in the world. This is why we need to get out of our Christian bubble.

But, how do we change this and learn to be like Jesus in the world today? Something that we see clearly in Scripture is that Jesus didn't barricade himself from society. The religious leaders clearly did, constantly avoiding the lowest of society, treating them like sinful scum. Jesus did the exact opposite, eating with uneducated fishermen, prostitutes, and tax collectors. If we want to be like Jesus, we need to get out of our Christian bubbles and engage the world head-on with the same love and power that He showed. Jesus engaged society by building relationships with those within the society. He did this by demonstrating His love for them through His actions and then teaching them about the kingdom through stories. This is our model of discipleship. This is how we go beyond "convert evangelism" and the "Christian bubble" to true disciple making. So, if you're wondering how you can best go and make disciples, the answer is simply by building relationships with the lost. It doesn't have to be big and dramatic like we sometimes make it out to be.

Chapter 29

A Place To Grow

When learning to love others, it is important to remember that the lost are not our only neighbors. When we become followers of Jesus, we enter into His Kingdom community. We actually become part of His family as I talked about in a previous chapter. This means that we have many brothers and sisters all across the world who make up the family of God. His family is called the Church. God's design for the church was for us to be a unified community made up of strong, growing relationships that centered around discipleship and growing in Jesus. Acts 2:44-47 describes what God desires the Church community to look like:

"Now all who believed were together, and had all things in common, and sold their possessions and goods, and divided them among all, as anyone had need. So, continuing daily with one accord in the temple, and breaking bread from house to house, they ate their food with gladness and simplicity of heart, praising God and having favor with all the people. And the Lord added to the church daily those who were being saved" (NKJV).

There are a few things that we can take away from this verse. These principles are important in how we build community together as the body of Christ in today's society, loving one another well. So many today believe that it isn't necessary to go to church to be a Christian. These principles that demonstrate what God's community should look like say otherwise.

1. They were together.

The most important thing to notice about the early church is that they did things together. The very definition of church signifies that. The word for Church in the original Greek that the New Testament was written in is the word *ekklēsia* which means "a gathering" or "an assembly."[1] Paul stresses the importance of gathering together in Hebrews 10:25 by saying that we should never stop gathering together (paraphrase). Being together is an important way that we build relationships that are based on love.

2. They had all things in common.

The next thing that we see about the early church was that they had all things in common, meaning that they were unified, sharing the same mindset about their life together. They all had experienced God's love and had chosen to respond to it by becoming disciples of Jesus and doing life together. They wanted to share their lives with each other because they had love for one another and a shared bond that centered around Jesus.

3. They took care of each other's needs.

I mentioned earlier that serving and meeting others' needs is a way to build a connection that leads to a healthy relationship. This is also a characteristic of the Church as demonstrated in Acts 2:45. We see that everyone in the Early Church sold their possessions and goods in order to provide for each other's needs. How many of us today would do this? Most of us don't pay tithes anymore, much less help support a missionary or give to the poor. We are too focused on providing for our own needs and wants. Most don't give out of either worry over finances or selfishness. However, this was never God's desire for the church. He wants every disciple of Jesus to take care of one another.

We must remember that serving is an important way to love others. If we don't serve others within the church, others who are supposed to be our family, how can we serve others who are lost and meet their needs? Serving and meeting needs in any way we can is one of the main ways we demonstrate the love that we have for others. This should be something that we naturally do as followers of Jesus.

4. They were together daily.

Something that I loved about campus ministry when I worked for Chi Alpha was the community culture that we developed with our students. I lived across the street from campus and I constantly had students come over. There would be times that they would spend all evening with my roommate and me talking about Jesus, eating, and playing games. Then they would come over the next day to hang out some more. I never grew tired of it, especially when those students truly grew in their faith because of those hang out sessions. There would be times when students came over to make brownies and then we would start talking about prayer and would pray until 3:00 or 4:00 in the morning. There would be times where we would have a game night and then someone would suggest that I get my guitar to have a worship session. Thirty minutes later they would be on the floor weeping in the presence of God, being filled with His Holy Spirit.

The early church looked very similar to this. The rest of this account in Acts 2 talks about how they gathered daily in the temple and in various houses across the city to learn, to eat, and to praise God and that God added to their numbers daily. We have lost this principle in today's church culture. We gather on Sunday morning to hear a sermon and sing a few songs and then leave, usually not speaking to one another throughout the week. Some don't even speak to other people in the church on Sundays, showing up late and leaving right after the service is done. This was never the way God designed the church to be.

BE THE CHURCH

If we want to love God and love others, showing the world that we are His disciples and representing Him well, we as the church must learn what true community is. We must learn to establish connections and build relationships with other believers where God has placed us. It all starts with love. Love that comes from God empowers and motivates us to build relationships with others and establish a thriving community. If we want to see the Church thrive in today's culture, we must practice this principle and discipline of building community. We must be the church, loving and serving one another as we grow in Christ together.

FERTILE GROUND

In another chapter, I mentioned that love is the breeding ground for growth and transformation. Community is how this occurs. Let me explain this further. I've said throughout the course of this book that God has a design for our lives, a divine plan that is filled with supernatural stories of His glory, transformation, and a destiny that has eternal reward. He empowers us to achieve this plan, teaching us to love Him and love others as we choose to become His disciples. Each of us has been created and empowered to do good works that He has uniquely designed us to do. However, there is one element that is necessary to accomplish the purpose for which we have been created. Picture this: a seed without ground cannot grow. Community is the ground where the seed of our purpose is planted. God did not create us to accomplish the good works that He created us for alone. A person without community cannot grow and cannot help others grow.

Let me put this bluntly: a Christian who does not go to church cannot understand how to follow Christ because they are not an active part of the body of Christ. Like plants who need fertile soil to survive, Christians need to be planted in the fertile soil of a church community. Those who are not planted in a church community are like plants who have been uprooted or planted in bad soil. They will never get the necessary nutrients. As a result, they are still in darkness because of their lack of knowledge and under-standing. Because they are still in darkness, they are still slaves to the things that hold them back. Because they have not established a healthy growing community with others, they cannot fulfill their purpose. They will never be able to love God with everything they are, and they will never understand how to love others as themselves. This is the simple truth. Jesus explains this very well in His parable of the sower in Matthew 13:3-8.

> "Behold, a sower went out to sow. And as he sowed, some seed fell by the wayside; and the birds came and devoured them. Some fell on stony places, where they did not have much earth; and they immediately sprang up because they had no depth of earth. But when the sun was up they were scorched, and because they had no root they withered away. And some fell among thorns, and the thorns sprang up and choked them. But others fell on good ground and yielded a crop: some a hundredfold, some sixty, some thirty" (NKJV).

Those who allow themselves to be planted in the fertile soil of a healthy church community that is filled with growing followers of Jesus will produce a crop that multiplies. Those who don't will be choked or never grow.

A PLACE OF GROWTH

There is one last principle that I want to emphasize as I bring this chapter to a close. Community is the ground where your purpose is planted. All throughout the last few chapters I have mentioned ways that God reveals His purpose to us, giving us a new identity as we respond to His love by becoming His disciples, empowering our natural gifts and abilities so that we can use them to do good works that He created us to do, as well as empowering us with His Holy Spirit to live a supernatural lifestyle with gifts that are beyond our ability. The thing that is important to remember, however, is that God has given us seeds that He wants us to plant. These seeds are part of who we are and come in the form of the talents He has given us to use. Without a place for these seeds to be planted in, they will never sprout and thrive. The community that we build is the ground where these seeds can be planted. When we go and do the good works that God has created us for, using our God given talents and abilities to help others grow in the community He has placed us in, we will thrive and achieve our destiny. Not only that, but because we used our talents and abilities to make disciples, others will thrive and achieve their destiny as well.

If you're wondering where God wants to plant you let me give you an answer: unless you have been given a supernatural calling to move locations, such as those who are called into missions or ministry in a different location, then the answer to where God wants to plant you is right where you are. You might have grown up in an area and decided to start a family there. You might have moved for a job that you felt like you were supposed to be in. You might have just liked a place and decided to move there. Whatever your reason for being there is, unless He says otherwise, wherever you are is where God wants to use you. That is where God has planted you. Grow and help others grow right where you are.

Something else that is important to remember is this: God entrusts people to you and expects you to help them grow. It's up to you to sow the seeds in their lives. Jesus emphasizes this principle in Matthew 3:13-16. He tells us, "

> You are the salt of the earth; but if the salt loses its flavor, how shall it be seasoned? It is then good for nothing but to be thrown out and trampled underfoot by men. You are the light of the world. A city that is set on a hill

cannot be hidden. Nor do they light a lamp and put it under a basket, but on a lampstand, and it gives light to all who are in the house. Let your light so shine before men, that they may see your good works and glorify your Father in heaven" (NKJV).

Let us always be the salt and light in others lives, planting the seeds in them that God has given us to sow. This is how we will accomplish the purpose that God has created us for and achieve our destiny.

Chapter 30

Shine Bright

I f we have love for God, He transforms us, empowering us continually so that we will never lose our flavor, allowing us to love people and be the light that shines bright. We shine bright by doing the good works we have been created to do in the community that He has placed us in. God entrusts His heart for the lost to us and expects us to do something with it. When we hide it, we are useless, but when we allow His heart to shine through us into others, they catch His heart as well. Multiplication happens, and the kingdom grows.

Ultimately, as lost people see our good works that we continually do because we love them, they will want to experience the same love that we have experienced, becoming Jesus's disciples as well. All it takes is asking the Holy Spirit to give us a love for the lost and for our brothers and sisters in Christ. Love shown through good works will help us establish a connection where discipleship can occur, and community can grow.

Billy Graham is one of the greatest evangelists known today. God entrusted him with a heart for people. He stewarded this well and people all over the world were impacted. Multiplication occurred, and the kingdom grew. What would have happened if he had hidden this precious gift God had given him? The millions of people who have given their lives to Jesus because of his ministry would still be in darkness if he had hidden what God had given him. This should be a challenge to all of us as followers of Jesus. Jesus gave us the gifts of salvation, light in the darkness, love, grace, and freedom as well as the tools we need to do the good works He has called us to do. He expects us to go and share them with others, seeing His kingdom multiply in the world around us. He also expects us to steward the lives He has given us well so that we can be as effective as possible in accomplishing the purpose He has given us. We will talk about that more in the next chapter. For now, I'll end this section the same way I began it. Building relation-ships and establishing a healthy growing community is one of the most important elements of discipleship. When we respond to God's love by becoming His disciples we are invited into God's community and given the responsibility of building relationships and community with both the lost and our fellow brothers and sisters in Christ. Only in community can we learn to truly be His disciples, using what God has given us to do good works, learning to thrive as God created us to, and ultimately fulfilling our purpose, loving Him with all of our being and our neighbor as ourselves.

Part 6 Steward Your Purpose

"walk worthy of the calling with which you were called"

Ephesians 4:1

Chapter 31

Keep Growing

A life following Jesus is a commitment to a life of growth. The very meaning of the word disciple implies growth. When we accept Jesus's invitation to follow Him, we accept His invitation to become His lifelong students, constantly learning new things as He broadens our understanding of who He is and our identity in Him. However, like I've said before in a different chapter, our life is filled with choices that will affect our growth. There will also be times where we don't know where to go or what to do. God asks us to follow Him even in those times, trusting in Him.

There have been times in my life where I felt that I had reached a point where I had stopped growing and had no idea how to continue to grow. One of those times was recently. As a worship leader I play several instruments including drums, guitar, and piano. Guitar is my primary instrument and I sing as well. I started playing when I was 18 years old and taught myself until I went to college and minored in traditional music. I learned a lot in this program, unlearning bad habits as a self-taught guitarist and becoming a more well-rounded musician. However, I made one crucial mistake. I only focused on what I wanted to learn rather than challenging myself to learn as much as I could have, limiting myself. Fast forward ten years later and I am still playing guitar the same way as I did in college and haven't progressed much in my musical knowledge. This has caused me to feel like I have plateaued musically. Unfortunately, much to my embarrassment, while I'm not content with where I am, I haven't done anything to progress further. I haven't had the necessary motivation to do so. Unfortunately, there are many who have the same mindset about their spiritual lives and relationships with others.

INVITED INTO THE EXTRAORDINARY

How many of us feel this way about different areas of our lives? We know we should be growing in specific areas, but don't feel motivated to do anything to grow. We settle for staying the way we are, content to live an average life or even less than average life in some cases.

However, we are not created to live an average or below average life, settling for being less than God intended us to be. God designed us for great things, as I've mentioned throughout this book. He calls us "New Creation" every day, giving us the power and strength to live out the identities He has for us. He calls each of us "Disciple of Jesus," "Child of God," "Heir of God," "More than Conqueror," and "His Workmanship," created to go make disciples and "do good works which God prepared beforehand that we should walk in them" (Ephesians 2:10, NKJV). He fills us with His Holy Spirit, empowering us to live the supernatural life that He has created us to live. When we walk in partnership with Him, He uses our natural gifts to make disciples and gives us supernatural gifts to go beyond our own abilities to grow His Kingdom community. He plants us in the community He wants us to be in, so that we can grow and help others grow, becoming the extraordinary people He has designed us to be, not just surviving, but thriving in every area of life.

Unfortunately, there are many people who are ok with just being ordinary. We make excuses like "I'm only human" or "I'm not perfect" so that we can keep on living the way we've always lived. However, this is a cop-out and an excuse that allows us to follow our own desires when we want, never fully submitting to the Holy Spirit. While we will never be perfect like Jesus, we can strive to be like Him in every area of life. You are designed in His image, created to be extraordinary, given what you need to go beyond fallen human limitations when you become His disciple. While this might be impossible on our own, we can do it with His help.

Jesus affirms this, saying, "with men this is impossible, but with God all things are possible" (Matthew 19:26, NKJV). You might say that it's impossible to be like Jesus and live an extraordinary, supernatural life like Him, but He says otherwise. Paul confirms this to us in Philippians 4:13 saying that "I can do all things through Christ who strengthens me" (NKJV). With His help we can live an extraordinary, supernatural life, thriving as He has designed us to thrive, filled with His Spirit, doing the good works that He has designed us to do, and accomplishing the purpose that He created us for. This is our destiny in Him.

All it takes is us accepting this fact and allowing love to motivate us to live the life He has designed for us. He is inviting us to experience His love in a way that motivates us to respond by becoming His disciples. When we follow Him, He helps us to love Him with everything that we are and love others as ourselves. This love motivates us to go and make disciples, doing good works, and building relationships in the community He plants us.

INVITED TO NEVER STOP GROWING

There is one principle that is extremely important to remember that will help us to never stop growing where He plants us. We will never know enough. There will always be something that we can learn as we follow Jesus. He is infinite, we are finite. He is omniscient, we are not. He is perfect, we are not. This principle is extremely important because there will be times where we might experience a season where we feel like we have plateaued and stopped growing. We might feel like there is nothing else we can learn. Pride can keep us stuck in this mentality if we are not careful, either in the form of arrogance or in the form of complacency. If we allow pride to get in the way of this principle we will stagnate and most likely experience our own destruction in some way, whether it be a moral failure, burnout, or falling because of our own arrogance.

God invites us to never stop growing in Him. This requires humility and discernment, especially during those times where we might feel like we have plateaued. If, instead of falling into pride, we remain humble and seek Him to discern the areas He wants to help us grow, He will reveal to us where He wants to take us next on the discipleship journey.

I'll use myself as an example. Like I mentioned in the beginning, there have been several instances in my life where I felt like I had plateaued, most recently being my own musical ability as a worship leader. It's been about ten years since I felt motivated to push myself to learn new things musically. Because of that, over the past year or two I have felt that I have been stuck in a creative funk. I have noticed that I've become frustrated where I am musically and in my own lack of growth as a worship leader. However, I also admit that I haven't had the motivation to try to learn more. I've focused more on other things such as writing and getting my master's degree. I also got married and started focusing on building a family. However, God spoke to me about this a few months ago saying this statement, "if you want to see others grow, you have to be growing as well. It's time to steward what I have given you, investing in your talents to see them grow so that you can invest into others."

As I have thought about this statement, it has opened my eyes to a deeper reality of God's design for our lives. God has given us everything that we have and wants us to use our lives and everything in them to grow His kingdom. However, we must steward our lives and what He has given us well so that we can invest what He has given to us into others and see His kingdom grow through us. That's what this chapter is about. God is inviting us into stewardship as His disciples.

Chapter 32

Stewardship

God is inviting us into a life of discipleship with Him. This life is filled with growth and transformation if we allow Him to transform us into the people He has called us to be. The plan He has for us is perfect and will allow us to thrive in every area of life. His plan will result in us experiencing eternal rewards if we choose to follow Him. He has called us to love Him and love others. We do this by accepting His invitation into discipleship and by doing the good works that He has designed us to do.

However, we must understand a very important principle. We are also called to keep on growing. To help us to keep growing, God is inviting us into stewardship. So, what is stewardship? The definition of stewardship according to the Merriam-Webster Dictionary is "the careful and responsible management of something entrusted to one's care."[1]

As Jesus's disciples we are "bought at a price" (1 Corinthians 6:20, NKJV). Our lives are not our own. We belong to God. However, because we still have free will even as His servants, we are still free to make our own choices with the lives He has bought. He doesn't demand our obedience. Instead, He gives us the choice to follow and obey Him. As His servants who have been set free from sin, we have been given the responsibility of stewarding or managing our lives. We can still make choices that limit us as His disciples, keeping us from living the extraordinary lives He wants us to live. It is our responsibility to live our lives "worthy of the calling" (Ephesians 4:1, NKJV) we have been invited into.

Stewardship is also how we accomplish the purpose that God has for our lives to love Him and love others. When we steward our lives well, living worthy of our calling, we love Him the way He wants us to, with all of our hearts, souls, and mind. When we don't, we show that we don't love Him as much as He wants us to. Stewardship also helps us to love others well, helping them grow as we grow. Like God told me about my musical ability, we can't help others grow unless we're growing as well. This is how we continue to do good works well.

So how do we live our lives worthy of the invitation He has extended to us? How do we steward our lives and what He has given to us well? There are a few principles that I'd like to talk about that will help us accomplish this purpose. An invitation to stewardship is an invitation into holiness, excellence, and to multiply what God has given you.

Holiness

Holiness is one of the most important characteristics of a follower of Jesus. Peter emphasizes this principle in 1 Peter 1:15-16 telling us, "but as He who called you is holy, you also be holy in all your conduct, because it is written, 'Be holy, for I am holy'" (NKJV).The Greek word that Peter used here is the word *agios* which means to be "a saint" or "pure, morally blameless, and consecrated."[2] He also refers to Leviticus 19:1 where God says to the children of Israel, "You shall be holy, for I the Lord your God am holy" (NKJV). The Hebrew word in this passage is the word *qāḏôš* which also means to be a saint, pure, and morally blameless but also means to be "set apart" and "sacred."[3]

God desires our lives and everything He gives us to be pure, morally blameless, consecrated, and set apart to be used for His purposes. He wants us to see our lives as sacred. This means that if we are to steward our lives well, we have to be holy and set apart from the ways of the world. Our lives can't look like the world. Like I mentioned earlier, too many of us, even as followers of Jesus, use the excuses of "I'm only human" or "I will never be perfect" to keep living like the world. An invitation to follow Jesus, loving God and people requires holiness. Accepting Jesus's invitation to discipleship requires us to steward holiness in our lives, not conforming "to the pattern of this world" (Romans 12:2, NIV), but instead presenting our bodies as a "living sacrifice, holy, acceptable to God" (Romans 12:1, NKJV). How do we steward holiness? By allowing the Holy Spirit to help us let go of the behaviors of the flesh that those in the world practice and instead practice walking in the fruit of the Spirit (Galatians 5:19-25).

We learn to do this by training our minds and hearts to focus "on things above, not on things on the earth" (Colossians 3:2, NKJV), meditating on "whatever things are true, whatever things are noble, whatever things are just, whatever things are pure, whatever things are lovely, whatever things are of good report, if there is any virtue and if there is anything praiseworthy" (Philippians 4:8-9, NKJV). Only when our minds and hearts are fully set on God, the truth, and walking in obedience to His will and plan can we be holy as He is holy. This is how we steward holiness in our lives. This is how we love God well and can help others love Him too. The good works that we do as we practice holiness allow us to reveal Jesus through our actions, helping others to see the truth and desire to follow Him themselves

Excellence

Another principle that allows us to steward our lives and what God has given us well is practicing excellence. Excellence is defined by Google as the "quality of being outstanding or extremely good." God desires us to be excellent, outstanding, and extremely good in all that we do. Paul emphasizes this in several verses. He tells the Corinthians to "excel in everything, in faith, speaking, knowledge, and in all earnestness and in the love we inspired in you" (2 Corinthians 8:7, NASB). He tells Titus, "in all things show yourself to be an example of good deeds, with purity in doctrine, dignified, sound in speech which is beyond reproach" (Titus 2:7, NASB). Paul also tells the Philippians to "approve the things that are excellent, that you may be sincere and without offense till the day of Christ" (Philippians 1:10, NKJV).

Understanding this principle of excellence and stewarding it well in your life helps you to do the good works that you have been designed to do "with all your might" (Ecclesiastes 9:10, NKJV). It also trains us to do these works for the Lord instead of men (Ephesians 6:7, Colossians 3:23, NKJV). Stewarding excellence helps us to "be sincere and without offense till the day of Christ, being filled with the fruits of righteousness which are by Jesus Christ, to the glory and praise of God" (Philippians 1:10-11, NKJV), proving our devotion to God because we are doing works excellently to demonstrate the sincerity of our love for Him and others (2 Corinthians 8:8).

Stewarding excellence in our lives, practicing being outstanding and extremely good in everything we do, also helps to put us in positions before others where our good works can shine and demonstrate God's power, bringing Him glory. Proverbs 22:29 says, "do you see a man who excels in his work? He will stand before kings; He will not stand before unknown men" (NKJV). Do you want to share the gospel before kings and people in positions of authority and influence? Do you want to build a community where you can see others come to Christ and make disciples as well? Steward excellence in your life, using everything He has given you with excellence to glorify Him and make Him known.

Multiplying

There is one last principle that I want to talk about that will help us steward our lives the way God wants us to. Let's go back to the statement that God told me when I was thinking about my own inability to grow musically. He told me this, "It's time to steward what I have given you, investing in your talents to see them grow so that you can invest into others."

As I have said throughout this book, God has given us natural and supernatural gifts that are a part of our calling. He wants us to use these gifts as ways to do the good works He has created us for. We can make disciples by using these abilities. However, like I mentioned in the last section, He wants us to practice excellence when using our abilities. This means that not only are we invited to use our talents to glorify the kingdom, but we are also called to grow those talents in order to bring Him more glory. Jesus gave a parable in Matthew 25:14-30 that demonstrates this principle:

"For the kingdom of heaven is like a man traveling to a far country, who called his own servants and delivered his goods to them. And to one he gave five talents, to another two, and to another one, to each according to his own ability; and immediately he went on a journey. Then he who had received the five talents went and traded with them, and made another five talents. And likewise, he who had received two gained two more also. But he who had received one went and dug in the ground and hid his lord's money. After a long time, the lord of those servants came and settled accounts with them. So, he who had received five talents came and brought five other talents, saying, 'Lord, you delivered to me five talents; look, I have gained five more talents besides them.' His lord said to him, 'Well done, good and faithful servant; you were faithful over a few things, I will make you ruler over many things. Enter into the joy of your lord.' He also who had received two talents came and said, 'Lord, you delivered to me two talents; look, I have gained two more talents besides them.' His lord said to him, 'Well done, good and faithful servant; you have been faithful over a few things, I will make you ruler over many things. Enter into the joy of your lord' Then he who had received the one talent came and said, 'Lord, I knew you to be a hard man, reaping where you have not sown, and gathering where you have not scattered seed. And I was afraid and went and hid your talent in the ground. Look, there you have what is yours.' But his lord answered and said to him, 'You wicked and lazy servant, you knew that I reap where I have not sown and gather where I have not scattered seed. So, you ought to have deposited my money with the bankers, and at my coming I would have received back my own with interest. So, take the talent from him, and give it to him who has ten talents. For to everyone who has, more will be given, and he will have abundance; but from him who does not have, even what he has will be taken away. And cast the unprofitable servant into the outer darkness. There will be weeping and gnashing of teeth'"(NKJV).

Let's break down this parable. The lord gives three servants money, expecting them to do something with it. God is the same. He gives us gifts in our lives that He expects us to use to make disciples excellently. There are three things in our lives that God entrusts to us: the time we have, the talents we have, and the treasures we have. Not only does God entrust them to us, but He expects us to steward these gifts well. We are to manage our time well, our talents well, and our treasures well. If we manage them well, letting them grow and shine, the things God gives us as part of the design He has for our lives can be useful in loving others and making disciples. Just like the two who invested their talents earned more, if we learn to steward these giftings well, investing in them to see them grow, using them to glorify God by investing into others to see them grow as well, we will be entrusted more. But if we hide them away, not managing them well, then those giftings are useless.

When we don't use what God has given us well, hiding ourselves instead of continually using and investing into the things God has given us, we become useless to the kingdom, just like the man who hid the talents. The Bible is very clear about what happens to those who are useless. They are thrown into the outer darkness. This should be a wakeup call to those who are not growing in Christ and responding to the invitation to go make disciples.

Stewarding the gifts that God has given us well and allowing them to shine as we invest into others allows us to effectively show the world who Christ is. Just like those who invested the talents in this parable experienced multiplication, the result of our investment and stewarding what God has given us well is a multiplication of our gifts and a multiplication of those who come into the kingdom,

Let's go back to my musical ability to illustrate this principle. I've mentioned that I'm a musician and worship leader. When God called me to be a worship leader, He didn't just download how to play guitar into my brain. He gave me a passion for music that grew as I practiced until I was able to play in front of people. But it didn't stop there. As I've followed Jesus, that talent has grown. I am now teaching others to lead worship as well, challenging them to grow in their giftings. What began with God entrusting me with a passion multiplied into an ability to teach others as well to be worship leaders and instilling that passion to lead people into the presence of God in others. However, as I mentioned in the beginning of this chapter, I have a sense that these abilities and passions have plateaued. I need to figure out how to grow so that others can grow. If I don't continue to steward my gifts well and keep investing into what God has given me so that I can grow, I will limit the growth in others that God wants me to help inspire. If I want to see excellence in others, I need to invest into myself so that others who I am leading and mentoring can grow as well.

Chapter 33

Stewarding Love

I want to talk about one more very important principle that is crucial in helping us steward our lives. As disciples of Jesus who have been given the purpose of loving God with all of our being and loving others as ourselves, we must learn to steward that love. What does stewarding love mean? What does it look like? Simply put, to steward love means we steward our relationships, making sure they are rooted and grounded in God's perfect love.

Love is the foundation for relationships, both with God and with others in our community. Without love we cannot have relationships. How do we steward our relationships, though? To answer this question let's go back to an earlier chapter and look at what love is and isn't.

Unlike what society says, love isn't just an emotion, it's a choice. It doesn't change based on circumstances and feelings. It's a lifestyle of putting others and God before ourselves. It's a lifestyle that only comes from experiencing God's love that "covers a multitude of sin" (1 Peter 4:8, NKJV), a perfect love that "casts out fear" (1 John 4:18, NKJV). It's a lifelong journey of saying yes to the invitation into discipleship with Jesus. Love is a lifestyle of putting others' needs in front of ours, a lifestyle that is full of patience, kindness, gentleness. It is a lifestyle of always rejoicing in the truth, believing the best of people, forgiving, showing grace and mercy, not being provoked to anger, bearing all things, believing all things, and enduring all things (1 Corinthians 13). This kind of love can only come as we follow Jesus. So how can we steward it?

Manage Your Emotions

Our emotions play a huge part in the decisions we make. It affects our ability to love. Emotions are a natural part of being created in the image of God. God Himself has emotions and created us to have them. The only difference between us and Him is that He has a perfect ability to control His emotions. His emotions do not affect who He is. We are the opposite. Sin has corrupted our emotions. Anger left unchecked can lead to hatred, unforgiveness, and bitterness. Our natural sexual desires left unchecked can lead to lust, sexual immorality, and adultery. Sadness and loneliness can lead to depression. The list can go on. The natural emotions that we were created with that are a part of who we are, have potential to turn into something that God did not design if we allow sin to keep them in bondage. Fortunately, God wants to redeem our emotions. He gives us a way to control and manage them with the help of the Holy Spirit.

Stewarding our emotions by becoming aware of them and managing them well is an important part of learning to steward love. In psychology, the degree of awareness a person has of their emotions is called emotional intelligence. The more aware a person is of their emotions and how they affect their decision making, the greater their emotional intelligence. The less aware, the lower their emotional intelligence. The greater your emotional intelligence is, the more mature you are.

As mature followers of Jesus, it is important to develop an awareness of our emotions and how they affect our ability to obey Him. For instance, we might get angry, but the more aware we are of our tendency to react negatively to anger the easier it will be to not react to that anger. We might have sexual desires, but if we are aware that looking at a man or woman with a shirt off might cause us to lust, we can avoid looking at those things that make us lust. We might be going through a situation that makes us sad, but if we understand that sadness isn't bad unless we allow it to rule us, we won't allow ourselves to go down into further depression. Do you get the point? We need to be aware of our emotions and how they affect us.

We also need to remember that the Holy Spirit is there to help us learn to manage our emotions. This is how we walk in the fruit of the spirit. With His help we can walk in peace in spite of feeling anxious, love in spite of having feelings of anger sometimes, joy in spite of feeling sad sometimes, self-control even in tempting situations, etc. The ability to steward your emotions with the help of the Holy Spirit is crucial for mature followers of Jesus. It is how we steward our relationships with others as well, walking in love instead of being controlled by emotions, reacting immediately to what others do instead of loving them, being patient, and showing them grace.

Manage Your Time

One of the gifts that God gives us is time. In human standards of time, we have 60 minutes in an hour, 24 hours in a day, 7 days in a week, 365 days in a calendar year. Each minute of the day and each day in the year needs to be managed well as a way of stewarding love. Relationships that are founded in love require setting time aside to do what is required to grow the relationship. What you do throughout the day to grow your relationship determines how healthy your relationships are. If you find that you are too busy for your relationships with God or others, then you are probably not stewarding the time that God has given you well. Learning to schedule your day and weeks, prioritizing what is most important before anything else, is how you steward your time, your relationships, and ultimately your love. How much time and effort you put into a relationship with God will be what you get out of it.

Manage Your Habits

We all have little tendencies that we constantly do unconsciously or consciously. These are called habits. For instance, I used to have a habit of putting my glasses down on the stand next to my bed every night and then knocking them off the stand the next morning, especially if I try to grab them in the dark. I have a habit of laughing at everything even if it's not funny. I have a habit of getting food all over me when I cook and eat, much to the annoyance of my wife. What habits do you have? I'm sure we can all think of hundreds.

Something I want us to consider, though, is that our habits need to be managed properly or they will affect our relationships. Habits can make or break a relationship. Let me explain a little further. A bad habit can ruin a relationship if it isn't stopped and replaced with a good habit. For instance, ignoring your spouse completely every day will most likely ruin a relationship. Yelling at your spouse when you're angry isn't helpful either. These might seem to be extreme examples, but I've seen these habits come out in couples several times in my life and none of them had healthy relationships. No matter what the habit is, if it's an unhealthy habit it will result in an unhealthy relationship. On the other hand, developing the good habits of showing love and patience to your spouse even when you're upset will help the relationship.

The same can be said of our relationships with God and others. Developing habits that are necessary for growing a good relationship is an important part of stewarding our lives and love for Him well. There are practical spiritual disciplines that we can implement into our daily lives that will help us develop new habits that will grow our relationship with God. These spiritual practices are prayer, reading Scripture, fasting, Sabbath rest, meditation, and praise and worship.

Prayer

Practicing daily prayer helps us develop the habit of praying "without ceasing" as Paul challenges us to do in 1 Thessalonians 5:17. Prayer is communication with God. Something that we sometimes miss about prayer is that it is two-way communication. Too many Christians today treat prayer as only asking God for help when we need it. They don't understand that prayer is not just about asking God for things. It's about developing a relationship with Him through talking as well as listening to Him. God wants to speak to us as well. As we develop this habit of communicating with God, we train our minds and hearts to recognize God's voice as He speaks to us. Prayer also helps us to learn the will of God as He shows us His plans and purposes for our lives. Practicing prayer helps us to steward our relationship with Him well.

Reading Scripture

Reading Scripture goes hand in hand with prayer. Scripture shows us who God is. It's His written word to us. It is how we learn who He is and how to become who He has called us to be. Developing the habit of reading Scripture helps us to develop the habit of thinking "on things above and not on things of the earth" (Colossians 3:2, NKJV). Reading and memorizing Scripture helps us to respond differently to sin and gives us the tools we need to resist temptation. We also have a better understanding of the truth by reading Scripture. When we develop the habit of reading Scripture, we train our minds to react to situations with the truth. In moments of temptation or weakness, the Holy Spirit will bring to mind the Scripture that we read that will help us to overcome and resist temptation and refocus on truth.

Meditation

Another spiritual discipline that will help us develop good habits that help us to steward our relationship with God is meditation. Meditation is, simply put, the practice of thinking about heavenly things. It goes hand in hand with reading Scripture because meditation is the action of thinking about and dwelling on the truth of Scripture. It can also be thinking about what God has spoken, keeping it fresh in our minds and hearts. Meditation helps focus our mind on God's presence and His word. It also helps us in times of anxiety to refocus our mind on truth and God's presence that brings peace, sadness to bring joy, anger to bring love and grace. When we develop the habit of learning to meditate, in good times and bad, we will remember His truth and refocus our attention on Him.

Sabbath

I talked about Sabbath rest in an earlier chapter, so I won't go too much into it in this chapter. Sabbath rest is simply learning to pause in our daily routines to refocus our attention on God. Developing this discipline can help us develop restful mindsets and habits even on the days that aren't Sabbath. Instead of getting anxious and over-whelmed, we can learn to rest in God's presence even when we're busy. Instead of getting distracted by things throughout the day we can learn to keep our attention on Him.

Fasting and Abstinence

Fasting is a spiritual practice that requires a lot of disci-pline. When we fast, we give up eating food for a period of time. It could be fasting lunch for a few weeks, fasting food for a whole day or for consecutive days. The purpose of fasting is to help us learn to crucify our flesh so that we can get more of God. "How does fasting help me develop better habits" you might ask. Fasting helps us to deny our fleshly desires. So, if your habit is to go to the fridge when you're sad, depressed, lonely, angry, etc and eat a bowl of ice cream, fasting can help you to develop the habit of turning to God instead. Fasting teaches us the discipline we need to not give in to the bad habits that we have and instead helps us control our emotions and flesh by turning to God.

Abstinence goes along with fasting in that it can give us better habits and help us focus on God more. When we abstain from something to focus on spiritual growth, we choose to give up something that was important to us so that we can focus on God more. For instance, I might give up and abstain from reading fiction books even if they're entertaining to read so that I can focus on reading books that are about spiritual growth. Both fasting and abstinence help us crucify fleshly habits and replace them with godly habits that help us grow in Him.

Praise

Praise is a spiritual discipline that is necessary to steward our love for God well. Praise turns our affections and attention away from ourselves and puts them on God. Praise helps us to remember who God is and what He has done, allowing us to develop the habits that Paul challenges us to make a part of our lives: "rejoice always," and "in everything give thanks" (1 Thessalonians 5:16,18, NKJV). Praise also puts God in a position of Lordship over our lives and helps us to keep our focus completely on Him, experiencing His presence that brings freedom. David says in Psalm 22 that God "is enthroned on the praises of His people." Another translation says that "He inhabits the praises of His people." When we praise Him, we put Him on the throne, making Him Ruler over our lives. This is why it's important to praise Him all the time. Some have the habit of only praising Him during the good times but blame Him in the bad. Some only turn to Him in the bad times and believe He isn't necessary in the good. However, He wants to be Lord of our lives in the good times and in the bad. He is the one who helps us in every season. It's through praise that He comes and gives us freedom, helping us to overcome. It's through praise that we remember that we can't do life on our own and that He is the one who helps us to thrive in every area of life. We must develop habits that allow us to praise Him even when we don't feel like it, helping ourselves remember that He is Lord and that He is always good, faithful, and kind. Praise allows us to continue to experience His love that leads us to repentance and helps us to grow.

Community

There is one more spiritual discipline that helps us to steward both our relationships with God and with others: community. Practicing community starts with establishing a connection with others, then grows when we actively try to grow the connection into a relationship. It requires intentionality and developing habits that will help us build a healthy relationship where discipleship can occur.

The habit that you can form to help steward the relationships in your life is to simply force yourself to talk to people in a way that helps build connection that leads to discipleship. You might be introverted, but if you force yourself to start building connections with people, you will get better at it and grow. You will learn what to say to them with the help of the Holy Spirit as you listen to Him. For extroverts, establishing connections is easy, but deep relationship building is sometimes harder. Extroverts tend to have a lot of friends, but none of them are especially deep friendships. The habit extroverts can develop is to simply learn to have one on one conversations that are deep rather than surface level. Instead of having lunch with a bunch of friends like extroverts love to do, you can invite one friend that you can have a time of conversation with that forces you to go deeper.

These habits of relationship and community building require intentionality as well as having a discipleship mind-set. If you want to see people become Jesus's disciples, build habits that help you be intentional about growing your community. This is how we steward love well as followers of Jesus.

PRACTICE MAKES PERFECT

God is inviting us to experience His love in a way that moti-vates us to respond by becoming His disciples. As we follow Him, He teaches us to love Him with all of our being and to love others as ourselves. We love others by making disciples, going and doing good works that we have been designed to do so that we can demonstrate our love. However, because we are fallen and prone to being distracted and plateauing in our growth, we must learn to steward what God has given us so that we can be faithful to His calling and keep growing.

However, stewardship isn't natural for us. We must practice disciplining ourselves in order to grow in maturity in every area of life. Paul describes our lives as a race. We must have the endurance to run it well. Stewarding our lives well so that we can run well takes practice. Paul describes how he stewards his life so that he can run the race well in 1 Corinthians 9:27. He says, "I discipline my body and bring it into subjection, lest, when I have preached to others, I myself should become disqualified" (NKJV). We need to learn to discipline ourselves as part of the stewardship process. We've all heard it said that "Practice makes perfect." The more we practice at stewarding what God has given us, doing the good works God has designed us to do well, the better we get at living life the way God intended us to. This is how we thrive and see the kingdom of God grow. This is how we accomplish the purpose God has given us of loving Him and loving others.

Conclusion

INVITED INTO WHOLENESS

As I draw this book to a close, I want us to ask this question: "What is my purpose?" Have you discovered yours yet? If you've read this book through its entirety and are still asking this question, keep reading. I'm going to summarize this entire book in this conclusion, hopefully helping you find an answer to what your purpose is.

As I've mentioned throughout this book, God has a plan and a purpose for our lives. It is a plan that is extraordinary and supernatural, leading us to an extraordinary destiny that has eternal reward. Understanding and discovering that destiny might be difficult unless we have a good understanding of calling. Calling is an invitation by God into partnership with Him. He knows each of our names and is inviting us on a journey with Him to find our purpose. This journey that He takes us on is part of a story of love that will blow the greatest stories of adventure and destiny that we hear out of the water.

On this journey He invites us to experience His love in

a way that allows us to find and achieve His purpose for our lives. He invites us to experience transformation as we learn to love Him as Lord, Father, and Friend. Along this journey we learn who God is through prayer and reading scripture, and through the community that He plants us in, allowing us to discover the identity that He has for us. We learn to be a "New Creation, "Disciple of Jesus," "Child of God," "Heir", "More than a Conqueror," and "His Workmanship." We learn that we are created to go make disciples, doing good works in the community that He plants us in as we love others as ourselves. Ultimately this journey leads us to our destiny.

OUR MAIN PURPOSE

So, saying all of that, what is our purpose? Here's the simple answer: our main purpose that God designed us all for is to love. He invites us to love Him with all our heart, mind, soul, and strength and to love others as ourselves. Did you catch that? I'll say that again. Your purpose is to love God and love others. Simple right? It is when we partner with Him and let Him help us that we can accomplish this purpose! This is what discipleship is all about, letting Him teach us how to love Him and love others.

When we discover how to love Him and love people, we will experience a deep wholeness like we have never experienced before. God's main intention as He plans our lives is to lead us to wholeness in Him, helping us to thrive in every area of our lives: spiritually, relationally, emotionally, mentally, physically, and financially. His well thought out design for our lives is for us to experience this wholeness in Him as we love Him and love people. As we follow His plan for our lives, He gives us the capability to thrive and succeed in everything that we do. However, the key to understanding this principle is this: we are in partnership with Jesus. Only with His help can we love Him and others, experiencing a wholeness that allows us to thrive.

Something to understand, though, is that loving God and loving people looks different for each of us. God has an individual, unique plan and purpose for each of us that helps us to accomplish our main purpose.

HIS UNIQUE PLAN

Because God created each of us to be different, we have our own unique characteristics and personalities that define who we are. God didn't make a mistake when He made us the way we are. He intended us to be different. Some of us are a little more different than others. I admit that I am one of those people. I'm pretty weird. However, I accept my differences. We all should. Our quirks are part of God's design.

He also has a well thought out plan for each of us, a plan for each of us to do "good works." As part of His plan, He creates each of us with unique characteristics and abilities that allow us to accomplish the good works that each of us was uniquely created for. God's intention for each of us is this: He wants to use what we already have been created with to go make disciples. He wants to use our hands, feet, voices, personalities, etc. to do good works that He designed us to do. He wants to use the passions and talents that He gave us to grow His kingdom and make disciples. When we allow Him to use what He created within us, going and making disciples by doing the good works we were designed to do, we demonstrate our love for Him and for others.

So, I'll ask this same question that I asked in an earlier

chapter: "what do you already possess that you can use to build God's kingdom?" If you have an ability to cook, use it to help others. If you have an ability to lead, lead others closer to God. If you have an ability to serve, serve well. If you have an ability to play music like me, join the worship team at your local church and lead others into God's presence. If you are a parent, parent well and lead your children to Jesus. If you're an aunt or an uncle, love your nieces and nephews and teach them about Jesus. Whatever it is that you love to do and are good at, do it for His glory and to build His kingdom.

Through the Holy Spirit's empowerment, God also gives us supernatural gifts that help us to do things that are beyond our abilities. These gifts help us live a supernatural life the way He wants us to live. These gifts help us to love Him and others well and are a part of His plans for our lives. As much as we might try, we aren't perfect and will always fall short even when we do use our natural abilities. We need His help to grow His kingdom. It's a partnership with Him. When we can't do something, He can. That's the beauty of the gospel.

When we learn to partner with God with the help of the Holy Spirit, He plants us each where He wants to use us. We are all called to go make disciples where He plants us. Some might be called to go overseas and do missions work, utilizing the ministry giftings that God has given them. Some might be called to do local ministry, also utilizing the ministry giftings that God has given them in a local context. Most,are called to go into the marketplace, using their giftings that God has given them within their chosen career. Wherever God has planted you, He has given you the ability to grow His kingdom wherever you are. It is your responsibility to accept His invitation and go and do the good works you were created to do to grow His Kingdom, making disciples as you do them. It is also your responsibility to grow yourself and others by stewarding excellence, holiness, and your relationships with God and others well. As you do this, you will experience wholeness in your life.

INVITED TO THRIVE

God's intention for us is to give us the ability to thrive in every area of life. He is inviting us into wholeness. However, to experience wholeness in our lives we must first experience His love that motivates us to become His disciples. When we become His disciples, the Holy Spirit comes into our lives, teaching us what it means to be His disciples. He transforms us, giving us a new identity and empowering us to do the good works that He has created us for.

Something for us to think about though is this: wholeness requires that we walk fully in God's plan. If there is one thing out of line, we will not be completely whole. That seems to be a little daunting doesn't it? What if we mess up? What if we don't understand God's will and plan completely? What if we get ahead of God's plan and accidentally do things our own way?

Here's the good news: God's grace is sufficient for us. It's a partnership with God. If wholeness required that we live a perfect life, never messing up, we'd be out of luck. Since we're not perfect, we'll never be whole, never able to thrive as God designed us to. God's grace and love fills the gaps where we are weak. Imagine our lives as an incomplete circle with gaps that need to be filled. The gaps are our weaknesses and shortcomings. God comes into those gaps and fills them with His grace and love, making us whole.

Here's something else to remember and be grateful for: it's ok to have gaps. It's those gaps that allow His glory to be made known in you and through you. He wants to fill your weakness with His strength so that He can get the glory from it. Accept your weaknesses but allow Him to make you strong. That's how you experience the wholeness He has for you. That is how you learn to thrive in every area of your life.

However, wholeness that allows us to thrive does require a few things from us:

1. It requires us understanding and accepting the identity He has for us as His disciples.
2. It requires us to be empowered by the Holy Spirit and to step out in faith doing the good works that He gives us the ability to do.
3. It requires us to go and make disciples.
4. It requires us being in community with others.
5. It requires us stewarding our lives as well as we possibly can with His help.

If you are missing even one of these requirements, you are not allowing Him to fill in the gaps in the circle of your life. His grace that fills the gaps in our lives requires us to surrender to His plan. When we don't step out in faith to follow Him and do these necessary things, we are following our own lesser plans, not His. He allows us to make our own choice to accept His grace or not. Without His grace filling your gaps, you will never be whole and will never understand and accomplish His perfect will and plan for your life. Without His help you will never thrive as He has designed you to do.

THE WILL OF GOD

Something that I've realized in my years of ministry is that when you're in the will of God, He will give you joy, peace, and a sense of excitement and security about the future, even if you don't understand what He's doing or know exactly where He's leading. This is what wholeness looks like. It's an ability to thrive and remain in God's peace, even when you don't know the future.

However, when you are not in the will of God, you will never have true contentment and will always be anxious and worried. Your mind will be in complete chaos. Sometimes we don't even know it, especially those of us who don't follow Jesus. The Bible refers to it as walking in darkness. Following Jesus and learning from Him is the only way to escape the darkness and walk in the light of truth and freedom. In the will of God is where you will find wholeness.

I experienced this a few years ago and it's what led to me writing this book. I've mentioned this testimony of the three-year season of discontent I went through a few times throughout this book. At the time, I was in a ministry role but wasn't emotionally healthy. I wasn't content with where I was in life and was struggling to find my place. I had become disillusioned and frustrated with everything, leading me down a path where I wandered in circles trying to figure out why I was frustrated. Fortunately, I was mature enough to turn to God in prayer and tried to keep a good perspective. However, I did a lot of things the wrong way. I neglected the friendships I had built in my community, preferring to be alone. I pursued relationships that I knew weren't the best, trying to find a spouse. I accepted ministry roles that I knew weren't part of God's plan for me trying to fill the hole left after I was forced to give up a dream.

All of the things I tried to do to find my purpose were actually distractions, keeping me bound to my own ways of doing things, trying to fill a void inside of myself that I didn't know I had. Fortunately, I didn't neglect my relationship with God, constantly praying for hours, fasting for days, trying to get Him to answer me and tell me what it was that I was supposed to do. I also asked for help from my pastor and a friend of mine who was a life coach.

However, I kept trying to do things my way instead of God's, deceiving myself into believing what I was doing was God's plan for me. It wasn't until I let go of everything that I heard God clearly and was able to discover that I had neglected the things that He had already created inside of me, trying to do things that I wasn't created to do. It was at this moment that God helped me to see how He wanted to use me to grow His kingdom. I needed to stop trying to be something I wasn't and just be who He had created me to be. I needed to let go of the identity I had created and just simply be His disciple.

It was in that moment of surrender that He renewed my vision and purpose. I started remembering what I have always loved to do and been fairly good at: writing, leading worship, and helping others discover who Jesus is and growing in their relationship with Him. He showed me that if I would use those things that I already had within me to make disciples He would use me. So, I started writing and growing in my talents. I got my master's in pastoral counseling. Ever since starting down this path of learning to just be the me He created me to be, He has revealed truths to me and strengthened my relationship with Him and others. I have experienced wholeness and growth in several areas of my life that I didn't realize were immature and broken. All it took was me letting go of my plans and saying yes to His design for my life.

How many of you have or know someone who has had similar experiences to mine? I hope you have found your purpose since reading this book and hearing my story. My goal with this book is to help everyone who reads it to discover their purpose and find wholeness. My desire is for you to thrive in every area of life. Learn to love God and love people. Learn what it means to be His disciple. Learn to steward what God has given you well. I hope this book will help you on your journey of learning to be like Jesus. Never stop growing and never stop surrendering. Never stop preaching the gospel and making disciples. Use your talents and passions to accomplish the calling that God has for you. Live in the identity that He has for you. Remember who He is and praise Him. Be continually empowered by the Holy Spirit to live a supernatural life. Walk with Jesus. There are people out there who need to hear what you have to say. They need to see Jesus through you. Be confident that He has called you and empowered you. Use your giftings to glorify Him. Build the kingdom in the way He has equipped you to. Live whole. Thrive in every area of life. Be like Jesus.

Notes

1. Destiny

1. "Purpose Definition & Meaning | Dictionary.Com." In *Dictionary.Com*, February 12, 2021. https://www.dictionary.com/browse/purpose.
2. "Definition of Destiny." In *Merriam-Webster Dictionary*, August 5, 2023. https://www.merriam-webster.com/dictionary/destiny.

2. The Perfect Plan

1. Blue Letter Bible. "H4284 - Maḥăšāḇâ - Strong's Hebrew Lexicon (Kjv)," n.d. https://www.blueletterbible.org/lexicon/h4284/kjv/wlc/0-1/.
2. "Definition of Peace." In *Merriam-Webster Dictionary*, August 6, 2023. https://www.merriam-webster.com/dictionary/peace.
3. Blue Letter Bible. "H7965 - Šālôm - Strong's Hebrew Lexicon (Kjv)," n.d. https://www.blueletterbible.org/lexicon/h7965/kjv/wlc/0-1/.

3. The Invitation

1. Blue Letter Bible. "G2564 - Kaleō - Strong's Greek Lexicon (Nkjv)," n.d. https://www.blueletterbible.org/lexicon/g2564/nkjv/tr/0-1/.

8. Invited Into Discipleship

1. "G3100 - Mathēteuō - Strong's Greek Lexicon (Kjv)." n.d. Blue Letter Bible. https://www.blueletterbible.org/lexicon/g3100/kjv/tr/0-1/.

9. Discipleship: The Story Of The Gospel

1. "G2564 - Kaleō - Strong's Greek Lexicon (Kjv)." n.d. Blue Letter Bible. https://www.blueletterbible.org/lexicon/g2564/kjv/tr/0-1/.

10. Discipleship: His Creative Power

1. "G1651 - Elegchō - Strong's Greek Lexicon (Nkjv)." n.d. Blue Letter Bible. https://www.blueletterbible.org/lexicon/g1651/nkjv/tr/0-1/.
2. Blue Letter Bible. "G3341 - Metanoia - Strong's Greek Lexicon (Kjv)," n.d. https://www.blueletterbible.org/lexicon/g3341/kjv/tr/0-1/.

14. The Renewed Mind

1. Blue Letter Bible. "G373 - Anapauō - Strong's Greek Lexicon (Kjv)," n.d. https://www.blueletterbible.org/lexicon/g373/kjv/tr/0-1/.
2. Blue Letter Bible. "H7673 - Šāḇaṯ - Strong's Hebrew Lexicon (Kjv)," n.d. https://www.blueletterbible.org/lexicon/h7673/kjv/wlc/0-1/.

17. Invited Into Identity

1. "G907 - Baptizō - Strong's Greek Lexicon (Nkjv)." n.d. Blue Letter Bible. https://www.blueletterbible.org/lexicon/g907/nkjv/tr/0-1/.
2. "G3686 - Onoma - Strong's Greek Lexicon (Nkjv)." n.d. Blue Letter Bible. https://www.blueletterbible.org/lexicon/g3686/nkjv/tr/0-1/.

18. New Names

1. Blue Letter Bible. "G5245 - Hypernikaō - Strong's Greek Lexicon (Kjv)," n.d. https://www.blueletterbible.org/lexicon/g5245/kjv/tr/0-1/.

19. Accept Your Identity

1. Blue Letter Bible. "H3372 - Yārē' - Strong's Hebrew Lexicon (Kjv)," n.d. https://www.blueletterbible.org/lexicon/h3372/kjv/wlc/0-1/.

2. Blue Letter Bible. "H6395 - Pālâ - Strong's Hebrew Lexicon (Kjv)," n.d. https://www.blueletterbible.org/lexicon/h6395/kjv/wlc/0-1/.

21. Your Part In God's Plan

1. Blue Letter Bible. "G2889 - Kosmos - Strong's Greek Lexicon (Kjv)," n.d. https://www.blueletterbible.org/lexicon/g2889/kjv/tr/0-1/.
2. Barna Group. "State of the Bible 2021: Five Key Findings - Barna Group," August 16, 2023. https://www.barna.com/research/sotb-2021/.

29. A Place To Grow

1. Blue Letter Bible. "G1577 - Ekklēsia - Strong's Greek Lexicon (Kjv)," n.d. https://www.blueletterbible.org/lexicon/g1577/kjv/tr/0-1/.

32. Stewardship

1. "Definition of Stewardship." 2023. In *Merriam-Webster Dictionary*. https://www.merriam-webster.com/dictionary/stewardship.
2. "G40 - Agios - Strong's Greek Lexicon (Kjv)." n.d. Blue Letter Bible. https://www.blueletterbible.org/lexicon/g40/kjv/tr/0-1/.
3. "H6918 - Qāḏôš - Strong's Hebrew Lexicon (Kjv)." n.d. Blue Letter Bible. https://www.blueletterbible.org/lexicon/h6918/kjv/wlc/0-1/.

Also by Benton J. Ward

Live It. BE It

About the Author

A licensed minister with the Assemblies of God, worship leader, life coach, and counselor with a Masters in Pastoral Counseling Benton Ward has a passion for discipleship and to help people thrive in every area of their lives. He loves to use his talents in writing, speaking, and leading worship to help others encounter God in a life changing way. He has served as a missionary with Chi Alpha Campus Ministries, as well as a worship pastor, young adults pastor, and youth pastor. He currently resides in Edinboro, Pennsylvania and serves as worship director of his home church Albion Assembly of God.

To contact Benton for speaking engagements, coaching/counseling sessions, etc, or to subscribe to his blog updates visit https://bentonjward.wixsite.com/benton jward. You can also visit his social media pages for updates and encouraging posts.

www.ingramcontent.com/pod-product-compliance
Lightning Source LLC
Chambersburg PA
CBHW071148130626
46553CB00004B/1575